C++

Table of Contents

C++ - A Beginner's Guide

C++ Tutorial for Beginners

C++ is an object-oriented language based on the C programming language. It can be viewed as a superset of C. Almost all of the features and constructs available in C are also available in C++. However, C++ is more than just an extension of C. Its additional features support the programming style known as *object-oriented programming.* Several features that are already available in C, such as input and output may be implemented differently in C++. In C++ you may use the conventional C input and output routines or you may use object oriented input and output by using the I/O Stream class library.

C++ was developed by Bjarne Stroustrup of AT&T Bell Laboratories. It was originally based on the definition of the C language stated in *The C Programming Language* by Brian W. Kernighan and Dennis M. Ritchie. This C language definition is commonly called *K&R C.* Since then, the International Standards Organization C language definition (referred to here as ISO/ANSI C) has been approved. It specifies many of the features that K&R left unspecified. Some features of ISO/ANSI C have been incorporated into the current definition of C++, and some parts of the ISO/ANSI C definition have been motivated by C++.

While there is currently no C++ standard comparable to the ISO/ANSI C definition, an ISO committee is working on such a definition. The draft of the Working Paper for Draft Proposed American National Standard for Information

Systems - Programming Language C+ +, X3J16/92-0091, is the base document for the ongoing standardization of C++. The IBM C and C++ Compilers adheres to the version of the ISO/ANSI working paper dated September 17, 1992.

This tutorial helps you to build your base with C++.

To whom this tutorial is designed for:

This book has been prepared for the beginners to help them understand the basic to advanced concepts related to C++.

Prerequisites:

Before you start practicing with various types of examples given in this tutorial,we are making an assumption that you are already aware of the basics of computer program and computer programming language.

C++ - Introduction

C++ is a statically typed, compiled, general-purpose, case-sensitive, free-form programming language that supports procedural, object-oriented, and generic programming.

C++ is regarded as a **middle-level** language, as it comprises a combination of both high-level and low-level language features.

C++ was developed by Bjarne Stroustrup starting in 1979 at Bell Labs in Murray Hill, New Jersey, as an enhancement to the C language and originally named C with Classes but later it was renamed C++ in 1983.

C++ is a superset of C, and that virtually any legal C program is a legal C++ program.

Note − A programming language is said to use static typing when type checking is performed during compile-time as opposed to run-time.

Object-Oriented Programming

C++ fully supports object-oriented programming, including the four pillars of object-oriented development −

- Encapsulation
- Data hiding
- Inheritance
- Polymorphism

Standard Libraries

Standard C++ consists of three important parts −

- The core language giving all the building blocks including variables, data types and literals, etc.

- The C++ Standard Library giving a rich set of functions manipulating files, strings, etc.

- The Standard Template Library (STL) giving a rich set of methods manipulating data structures, etc.

The ANSI Standard

The ANSI standard is an attempt to ensure that C++ is portable; that code you write for Microsoft's compiler will compile without errors, using a compiler on a Mac, UNIX, a Windows box, or an Alpha.

The ANSI standard has been stable for a while, and all the major C++ compiler manufacturers support the ANSI standard.

Learning C++

The most important thing while learning C++ is to focus on concepts.

The purpose of learning a programming language is to become a better programmer; that is, to become more effective at designing and implementing new systems and at maintaining old ones.

C++ supports a variety of programming styles. You can write in the style of Fortran, C, Smalltalk, etc., in any language. Each style can achieve its aims effectively while maintaining runtime and space efficiency.

Use of C++

C++ is used by hundreds of thousands of programmers in essentially every application domain.

C++ is being highly used to write device drivers and other software that rely on direct manipulation of hardware under realtime constraints.

C++ is widely used for teaching and research because it is clean enough for successful teaching of basic concepts.

Anyone who has used either an Apple Macintosh or a PC running Windows has indirectly used C++ because the primary user interfaces of these systems are written in C++.

C++ Environment Setup

Local Environment Setup:

If you are still willing to set up your environment for C++, you need to have the following two software's on your computer.

Text Editor

This will be used to type your program. Examples of few editors include Windows Notepad, OS Edit command, Brief, Epsilon, EMACS, and vim or vi.

Name and version of text editor can vary on different operating systems. For example, Notepad will be used on Windows and vim or vi can be used on windows as well as Linux, or UNIX.

The files you create with your editor are called source files and for C++ they typically are named with the extension .cpp, .cp, or .c.

A text editor should be in place to start your C++ programming.

C++ Compiler

This is an actual C++ compiler, which will be used to compile your source code into final executable program.

Most C++ compilers don't care what extension you give to your source code, but if you don't specify otherwise, many will use .cpp by default.

Most frequently used and free available compiler is GNU C/C++ compiler, otherwise you can have compilers either from HP or Solaris if you have the respective Operating Systems.

Installing GNU C/C++ Compiler:

UNIX/Linux Installation

If you are using **Linux or UNIX** then check whether GCC is installed on your system by entering the following command from the command line −

$ g++ -v

If you have installed GCC, then it should print a message such as the following −

Using built-in specs.
Target: i386-redhat-linux
Configured with: ../configure --prefix=/usr ....
Thread model: posix
gcc version 4.1.2 20080704 (Red Hat 4.1.2-46)

If GCC is not installed, then you will have to install it yourself using the detailed instructions available at https://gcc.gnu.org/install/

Mac OS X Installation

If you use Mac OS X, the easiest way to obtain GCC is to download the Xcode development environment from

Apple's website and follow the simple installation instructions.

Xcode is currently available at

developer.apple.com/technologies/tools/.

Windows Installation

To install GCC at Windows you need to install MinGW. To install MinGW, go to the MinGW homepage, www.mingw.org, and follow the link to the MinGW download page. Download the latest version of the MinGW installation program which should be named MinGW-<version>.exe.

While installing MinGW, at a minimum, you must install gcc-core, gcc-g++, binutils, and the MinGW runtime, but you may wish to install more.

Add the bin subdirectory of your MinGW installation to your **PATH** environment variable so that you can specify these tools on the command line by their simple names.

When the installation is complete, you will be able to run gcc, g++, ar, ranlib, dlltool, and several other GNU tools from the Windows command line.

C++ Basic Syntax

When we consider a C++ program, it can be defined as a collection of objects that communicate via invoking each other's methods. Let us now briefly look into what a class, object, methods, and instant variables mean.

- **Object** – Objects have states and behaviors. Example: A dog has states - color, name, breed as well as behaviors - wagging, barking, eating. An object is an instance of a class.

- **Class** – A class can be defined as a template/blueprint that describes the behaviors/states that object of its type support.

- **Methods** – A method is basically a behavior. A class can contain many methods. It is in methods where the logics are written, data is manipulated and all the actions are executed.

- **Instance Variables** – Each object has its unique set of instance variables. An object's state is created by the values assigned to these instance variables.

C++ Program Structure

Let us look at a simple code that would print the words *Hello World*.

```
#include <iostream>
using namespace std;

// main() is where program execution begins.
```

```
int main() {
  cout << "Hello World"; // prints Hello World
  return 0;
}
```

Let us look at the various parts of the above program −

- The C++ language defines several headers, which contain information that is either necessary or useful to your program. For this program, the header **<iostream>** is needed.

- The line **using namespace std;** tells the compiler to use the std namespace. Namespaces are a relatively recent addition to C++.

- The next line '// **main() is where program execution begins.**' is a single-line comment available in C++. Single-line comments begin with // and stop at the end of the line.

- The line **int main()** is the main function where program execution begins.

- The next line **cout << "Hello World";** causes the message "Hello World" to be displayed on the screen.

- The next line **return 0;** terminates main( )function and causes it to return the value 0 to the calling process.

Compile and Execute C++ Program

Let's look at how to save the file, compile and run the program. Please follow the steps given below −

- Open a text editor and add the code as above.

- Save the file as: hello.cpp

- Open a command prompt and go to the directory where you saved the file.

- Type 'g++ hello.cpp' and press enter to compile your code. If there are no errors in your code the command prompt will take you to the next line and would generate a.out executable file.

- Now, type 'a.out' to run your program.

- You will be able to see ' Hello World ' printed on the window.

```
$ g++ hello.cpp
$ ./a.out
Hello World
```

Make sure that g++ is in your path and that you are running it in the directory containing file hello.cpp.

You can compile C/C++ programs using unix makefile.

Semicolons and Blocks in C++

In C++, the semicolon is a statement terminator. That is, each individual statement must be ended with a semicolon. It indicates the end of one logical entity.

For example, following are three different statements −

```
x = y;
y = y + 1;
add(x, y);
```

A block is a set of logically connected statements that are surrounded by opening and closing braces.

For example −

```
{
  cout << "Hello World"; // prints Hello World
  return 0;
}
```

C++ does not recognize the end of the line as a terminator. For this reason, it does not matter where you put a statement in a line. For example −

```
x = y;
y = y + 1;
add(x, y);
```

is the same as

```
x = y; y = y + 1; add(x, y);
```

C++ Identifiers

A C++ identifier is a name used to identify a variable, function, class, module, or any other user-defined item. An identifier starts with a letter A to Z or a to z or an underscore (_) followed by zero or more letters, underscores, and digits (0 to 9).

C++ does not allow punctuation characters such as @, $, and % within identifiers. C++ is a case-sensitive programming language.

Thus, **Manpower** and **manpower** are two different identifiers in C++.

Here are some examples of acceptable identifiers −

```
mohd    zara   abc  move_name a_123
myname50 _temp j   a23b9    retVal
```

C++ Keywords

The following list shows the reserved words in C++. These reserved words may not be used as constant or variable or any other identifier names.

asm	else	new	this
auto	enum	operator	throw
bool	explicit	private	true
break	export	protected	try
case	extern	public	typedef
catch	false	register	typeid
char	float	reinterpret_cast	typename
class	for	return	union
const	friend	short	unsigned

const_cast	goto	signed	using
continue	if	sizeof	virtual
default	inline	static	void
delete	int	static_cast	volatile
do	long	struct	wchar_t
double	mutable	switch	while
dynamic_cast	namespace	template	

Trigraphs

A few characters have an alternative representation, called a trigraph sequence. A trigraph is a three-character sequence that represents a single character and the sequence always starts with two question marks.

Trigraphs are expanded anywhere they appear, including within string literals and character literals, in comments, and in preprocessor directives.

Following are most frequently used trigraph sequences −

Trigraph	Replacement
??=	#
??/	\
??'	^
??(	[
??)	]
??!	|
??<	{
??>	}
??-	~

All the compilers do not support trigraphs and they are not advised to be used because of their confusing nature.

Whitespace in C++

A line containing only whitespace, possibly with a comment, is known as a blank line, and C++ compiler totally ignores it.

Whitespace is the term used in C++ to describe blanks, tabs, newline characters and comments. Whitespace separates one part of a statement from another and enables the compiler to identify where one element in a statement, such as int, ends and the next element begins.

Statement 1

int age;

In the above statement there must be at least one whitespace character (usually a space) between int and age for the compiler to be able to distinguish them.

Statement 2

fruit = apples + oranges;   // Get the total fruit

In the above statement 2, no whitespace characters are necessary between fruit and =, or between = and apples, although you are free to include some if you wish for readability purpose.

Comments in C++:

Program comments are explanatory statements that you can include in the C++ code. These comments help anyone reading the source code. All programming languages allow for some form of comments.

C++ supports single-line and multi-line comments.

All characters available inside any comment are ignored by C++ compiler.

C++ comments start with /* and end with */.

For example −

```
/* This is a comment */

/* C++ comments can also
 * span multiple lines
 */
```

A comment can also start with //, extending to the end of the line.

For example −

```
#include <iostream>
using namespace std;

main() {
   cout << "Hello World"; // prints Hello World

   return 0;
}
```

When the above code is compiled, it will ignore // **prints Hello World** and final executable will produce the following result −

```
Hello World
```

Within a /* and */ comment, // characters have no special meaning.

Within a // comment, /* and */ have no special meaning. Thus, you can "nest" one kind of comment within the other kind.

For example −

```
/* Comment out printing of Hello World:

cout << "Hello World"; // prints Hello World

*/
```

C++ Data Types

While writing program in any language, you need to use various variables to store various information. Variables are nothing but reserved memory locations to store values. This means that when you create a variable you reserve some space in memory.

You may like to store information of various data types like character, wide character, integer, floating point, double floating point, boolean etc. Based on the data type of a variable, the operating system allocates memory and decides what can be stored in the reserved memory.

Primitive Built-in Types

C++ offers the programmer a rich assortment of built-in as well as user defined data types. Following table lists down seven basic C++ data types –

Type	Keyword
Boolean	bool
Character	char
Integer	int

Floating point	float
Double floating point	double
Valueless	void
Wide character	wchar_t

Several of the basic types can be modified using one or more of these type modifiers −

- signed
- unsigned
- short
- long

The following table shows the variable type, how much memory it takes to store the value in memory, and what is maximum and minimum value which can be stored in such type of variables.

Type	Typical Bit Width	Typical Range
char	1byte	-127 to 127 or 0 to 255

unsigned char	1byte	0 to 255
signed char	1byte	-127 to 127
int	4bytes	-2147483648 to 2147483647
unsigned int	4bytes	0 to 4294967295
signed int	4bytes	-2147483648 to 2147483647
short int	2bytes	-32768 to 32767
unsigned short int	Range	0 to 65,535
signed short int	Range	-32768 to 32767
long int	4bytes	-2,147,483,648 to 2,147,483,647

signed long int	4bytes	same as long int
unsigned long int	4bytes	0 to 4,294,967,295
float	4bytes	+/- 3.4e +/- 38 (~7 digits)
double	8bytes	+/- 1.7e +/- 308 (~15 digits)
long double	8bytes	+/- 1.7e +/- 308 (~15 digits)
wchar_t	2 or 4 bytes	1 wide character

The size of variables might be different from those shown in the above table, depending on the compiler and the computer you are using.

Following is the example, which will produce correct size of various data types on your computer.

```cpp
#include <iostream>
using namespace std;
```

```
int main() {
  cout << "Size of char : " << sizeof(char) << endl;
  cout << "Size of int : " << sizeof(int) << endl;
  cout << "Size of short int : " << sizeof(short int) << endl;
  cout << "Size of long int : " << sizeof(long int) << endl;
  cout << "Size of float : " << sizeof(float) << endl;
  cout << "Size of double : " << sizeof(double) << endl;
  cout << "Size of wchar_t : " << sizeof(wchar_t) << endl;

  return 0;
}
```

This example uses **endl**, which inserts a new-line character after every line and << operator is being used to pass multiple values out to the screen. We are also using **sizeof()** operator to get size of various data types.

When the above code is compiled and executed, it produces the following result which can vary from machine to machine –

```
Size of char : 1
Size of int : 4
Size of short int : 2
Size of long int : 4
Size of float : 4
Size of double : 8
Size of wchar_t : 4
```

typedef Declarations:

You can create a new name for an existing type using **typedef**. Following is the simple syntax to define a new type using typedef –

typedef type newname;

For example, the following tells the compiler that feet is another name for int –

typedef int feet;

Now, the following declaration is perfectly legal and creates an integer variable called distance –

feet distance;

Enumerated Types:

An enumerated type declares an optional type name and a set of zero or more identifiers that can be used as values of the type. Each enumerator is a constant whose type is the enumeration.

Creating an enumeration requires the use of the keyword **enum**. The general form of an enumeration type is –

enum enum-name { list of names } var-list;

Here, the enum-name is the enumeration's type name. The list of names is comma separated.

For example, the following code defines an enumeration of colors called colors and the variable c of type color. Finally, c is assigned the value "blue".

```
enum color { red, green, blue } c;
c = blue;
```

By default, the value of the first name is 0, the second name has the value 1, and the third has the value 2, and so on. But you can give a name, a specific value by adding an initializer.

For example, in the following enumeration, **green** will have the value 5.

```
enum color { red, green = 5, blue };
```

Here, **blue** will have a value of 6 because each name will be one greater than the one that precedes it.

C++ Variable Types

A variable provides us with named storage that our programs can manipulate. Each variable in C++ has a specific type, which determines the size and layout of the variable's memory; the range of values that can be stored within that memory; and the set of operations that can be applied to the variable.

The name of a variable can be composed of letters, digits, and the underscore character. It must begin with either a letter or an underscore. Upper and lowercase letters are distinct because C++ is case-sensitive −

There are following basic types of variable in C++ as explained in last chapter −

Sr.No	Type & Description
1	**bool** Stores either value true or false.
2	**char** Typically a single octet (one byte). This is an integer type.
3	**int** The most natural size of integer for the machine.

4	**float** A single-precision floating point value.
5	**double** A double-precision floating point value.
6	**void** Represents the absence of type.
7	**wchar_t** A wide character type.

C++ also allows to define various other types of variables, which we will cover in subsequent chapters like **Enumeration, Pointer, Array, Reference, Data structures,**and **Classes**.

Following section will cover how to define, declare and use various types of variables.

Variable Definition in C++:

A variable definition tells the compiler where and how much storage to create for the variable. A variable definition specifies a data type, and contains a list of one or more variables of that type as follows −

```
type variable_list;
```

Here, **type** must be a valid C++ data type including char, w_char, int, float, double, bool or any user-defined object, etc., and **variable_list** may consist of one or more identifier names separated by commas. Some valid declarations are shown here –

```
int   i, j, k;
char  c, ch;
float f, salary;
double d;
```

The line **int i, j, k;** both declares and defines the variables i, j and k; which instructs the compiler to create variables named i, j and k of type int.

Variables can be initialized (assigned an initial value) in their declaration. The initializer consists of an equal sign followed by a constant expression as follows –

```
type variable_name = value;
```

Some examples are –

```
extern int d = 3, f = 5;   // declaration of d and f.
int d = 3, f = 5;          // definition and initializing d and f.
byte z = 22;               // definition and initializes z.
char x = 'x';              // the variable x has the value 'x'.
```

For definition without an initializer: variables with static storage duration are implicitly initialized with NULL (all bytes have the value 0); the initial value of all other variables is undefined.

Variable Declaration in C++:

A variable declaration provides assurance to the compiler that there is one variable existing with the given type and name so that compiler proceed for further compilation without needing complete detail about the variable. A variable declaration has its meaning at the time of compilation only, compiler needs actual variable definition at the time of linking of the program.

A variable declaration is useful when you are using multiple files and you define your variable in one of the files which will be available at the time of linking of the program. You will use **extern** keyword to declare a variable at any place. Though you can declare a variable multiple times in your C++ program, but it can be defined only once in a file, a function or a block of code.

Example

Try the following example where a variable has been declared at the top, but it has been defined inside the main function −

```cpp
#include <iostream>
using namespace std;

// Variable declaration:
extern int a, b;
extern int c;
extern float f;

int main () {
   // Variable definition:
   int a, b;
   int c;
   float f;

   // actual initialization
   a = 10;
   b = 20;
```

```
c = a + b;

cout << c << endl ;

f = 70.0/3.0;
cout << f << endl ;

return 0;
}
```

When the above code is compiled and executed, it produces the following result –

```
30
23.3333
```

Same concept applies on function declaration where you provide a function name at the time of its declaration and its actual definition can be given anywhere else. For example –

```
// function declaration
int func();
int main() {
  // function call
  int i = func();
}

// function definition
int func() {
  return 0;
}
```

Lvalues and Rvalues

There are two kinds of expressions in C++ −

- **lvalue** − Expressions that refer to a memory location is called "lvalue" expression. An lvalue may appear as either the left-hand or right-hand side of an assignment.

- **rvalue** − The term rvalue refers to a data value that is stored at some address in memory. An rvalue is an expression that cannot have a value assigned to it which means an rvalue may appear on the right- but not left-hand side of an assignment.

Variables are lvalues and so may appear on the left-hand side of an assignment. Numeric literals are rvalues and so may not be assigned and can not appear on the left-hand side. Following is a valid statement −

int g = 20;

But the following is not a valid statement and would generate compile-time error −

10 = 20;

Variable Scope in C++:

A scope is a region of the program and broadly speaking there are three places, where variables can be declared −

- Inside a function or a block which is called local variables,

- In the definition of function parameters which is called formal parameters.

- Outside of all functions which is called global variables.

We will learn what is a function and it's parameter in subsequent chapters. Here let us explain what are local and global variables.

Local Variables:

Variables that are declared inside a function or block are local variables. They can be used only by statements that are inside that function or block of code. Local variables are not known to functions outside their own. Following is the example using local variables −

```cpp
#include <iostream>
using namespace std;

int main () {
   // Local variable declaration:
   int a, b;
   int c;

   // actual initialization
   a = 10;
   b = 20;
   c = a + b;

   cout << c;

   return 0;
}
```

Global Variables:

Global variables are defined outside of all the functions, usually on top of the program. The global variables will hold their value throughout the life-time of your program.

A global variable can be accessed by any function. That is, a global variable is available for use throughout your entire program after its declaration.

Following is the example using global and local variables –

```cpp
#include <iostream>
using namespace std;

// Global variable declaration:
int g;

int main () {
   // Local variable declaration:
   int a, b;

   // actual initialization
   a = 10;
   b = 20;
   g = a + b;

   cout << g;

   return 0;
}
```

A program can have same name for local and global variables but value of local variable inside a function will take preference.

For example −

```
#include <iostream>
using namespace std;

// Global variable declaration:
int g = 20;

int main () {
   // Local variable declaration:
   int g = 10;

   cout << g;

   return 0;
}
```

When the above code is compiled and executed, it produces the following result −

10

Initializing Local and Global Variables:

When a local variable is defined, it is not initialized by the system, you must initialize it yourself.

Global variables are initialized automatically by the system when you define them as follows −

Data Type	Initializer
int	0

char	'\0'
float	0
double	0
pointer	NULL

It is a good programming practice to initialize variables properly, otherwise sometimes program would produce unexpected result.

C++ Constants/Literals

Constants refer to fixed values that the program may not alter and they are called **literals**.

Constants can be of any of the basic data types and can be divided into Integer Numerals, Floating-Point Numerals, Characters, Strings and Boolean Values.

Again, constants are treated just like regular variables except that their values cannot be modified after their definition.

Integer Literals:

An integer literal can be a decimal, octal, or hexadecimal constant. A prefix specifies the base or radix: 0x or 0X for hexadecimal, 0 for octal, and nothing for decimal.

An integer literal can also have a suffix that is a combination of U and L, for unsigned and long, respectively. The suffix can be uppercase or lowercase and can be in any order.

Here are some examples of integer literals –

```
212      // Legal
215u     // Legal
0xFeeL   // Legal
078      // Illegal: 8 is not an octal digit
032UU    // Illegal: cannot repeat a suffix
```

Following are other examples of various types of Integer literals –

```
85      // decimal
```

```
0213    // octal
0x4b    // hexadecimal
30      // int
30u     // unsigned int
30l     // long
30ul    // unsigned long
```

Floating-point Literals:

A floating-point literal has an integer part, a decimal point, a fractional part, and an exponent part. You can represent floating point literals either in decimal form or exponential form.

While representing using decimal form, you must include the decimal point, the exponent, or both and while representing using exponential form, you must include the integer part, the fractional part, or both. The signed exponent is introduced by e or E.

Here are some examples of floating-point literals –

```
3.14159     // Legal
314159E-5L  // Legal
510E        // Illegal: incomplete exponent
210f        // Illegal: no decimal or exponent
.e55        // Illegal: missing integer or fraction
```

Boolean Literals

There are two Boolean literals and they are part of standard C++ keywords –

- A value of **true** representing true.

- A value of **false** representing false.

You should not consider the value of true equal to 1 and value of false equal to 0.

Character Literals

Character literals are enclosed in single quotes. If the literal begins with L (uppercase only), it is a wide character literal (e.g., L'x') and should be stored in **wchar_t** type of variable . Otherwise, it is a narrow character literal (e.g., 'x') and can be stored in a simple variable of **char** type.

A character literal can be a plain character (e.g., 'x'), an escape sequence (e.g., '\t'), or a universal character (e.g., '\u02C0').

There are certain characters in C++ when they are preceded by a backslash they will have special meaning and they are used to represent like newline (\n) or tab (\t). Here, you have a list of some of such escape sequence codes −

Escape sequence	Meaning
\\	\ character
\'	' character
\"	" character

\?	? character
\a	Alert or bell
\b	Backspace
\f	Form feed
\n	Newline
\r	Carriage return
\t	Horizontal tab
\v	Vertical tab
\ooo	Octal number of one to three digits
\xhh . . .	Hexadecimal number of one or more digits

Following is the example to show a few escape sequence characters –

```cpp
#include <iostream>
using namespace std;

int main() {
    cout << "Hello\tWorld\n\n";
    return 0;
}
```

When the above code is compiled and executed, it produces the following result –

Hello   World

String Literals

String literals are enclosed in double quotes. A string contains characters that are similar to character literals: plain characters, escape sequences, and universal characters.

You can break a long line into multiple lines using string literals and separate them using whitespaces.

Here are some examples of string literals. All the three forms are identical strings.

```cpp
"hello, dear"

"hello, \

dear"

"hello, " "d" "ear"
```

Defining Constants:

There are two simple ways in C++ to define constants −

- Using **#define** preprocessor.
- Using **const** keyword.

The #define Preprocessor

Following is the form to use #define preprocessor to define a constant −

```
#define identifier value
```

Following example explains it in detail −

```cpp
#include <iostream>
using namespace std;

#define LENGTH 10
#define WIDTH  5
#define NEWLINE '\n'

int main() {
   int area;

   area = LENGTH * WIDTH;
   cout << area;
   cout << NEWLINE;
   return 0;
}
```

When the above code is compiled and executed, it produces the following result −

The const Keyword

You can use **const** prefix to declare constants with a specific type as follows –

const type variable = value;

Following example explains it in detail –

```cpp
#include <iostream>
using namespace std;

int main() {
   const int  LENGTH = 10;
   const int  WIDTH  = 5;
   const char NEWLINE = '\n';
   int area;

   area = LENGTH * WIDTH;
   cout << area;
   cout << NEWLINE;
   return 0;
}
```

When the above code is compiled and executed, it produces the following result –

50

Note that it is a good programming practice to define constants in CAPITALS.

C++ Modifier Types

C++ allows the **char, int,** and **double** data types to have modifiers preceding them. A modifier is used to alter the meaning of the base type so that it more precisely fits the needs of various situations.

The data type modifiers are listed here −

- signed
- unsigned
- long
- short

The modifiers **signed, unsigned, long,** and **short** can be applied to integer base types. In addition, **signed** and **unsigned** can be applied to char, and **long** can be applied to double.

The modifiers **signed** and **unsigned** can also be used as prefix to **long** or **short**modifiers. For example, **unsigned long int**.

C++ allows a shorthand notation for declaring **unsigned, short,** or **long** integers. You can simply use the word **unsigned,** **short,** or **long,** without **int**. It automatically implies **int**. For example, the following two statements both declare unsigned integer variables.

```
unsigned x;
unsigned int y;
```

To understand the difference between the way signed and unsigned integer modifiers are interpreted by C++, you should run the following short program −

```
#include <iostream>
using namespace std;

/* This program shows the difference between
 * signed and unsigned integers.
 */
int main() {
    short int i;          // a signed short integer
    short unsigned int j; // an unsigned short integer

    j = 50000;

    i = j;
    cout << i << " " << j;

    return 0;
}
```

When this program is run, following is the output −

-15536 50000

The above result is because the bit pattern that represents 50,000 as a short unsigned integer is interpreted as -15,536 by a short.

Type Qualifiers in C++

The type qualifiers provide additional information about the variables they precede.

Sr.No	Qualifier & Meaning
1	**const** Objects of type **const** cannot be changed by your program during execution.
2	**volatile** The modifier **volatile** tells the compiler that a variable's value may be changed in ways not explicitly specified by the program.
3	**restrict** A pointer qualified by **restrict** is initially the only means by which the object it points to can be accessed. Only C99 adds a new type qualifier called restrict.

Storage Classes in C++:

A storage class defines the scope (visibility) and life-time of variables and/or functions within a C++ Program. These specifiers precede the type that they modify. There are following storage classes, which can be used in a C++ Program

- auto
- register
- static

- extern
- mutable

The auto Storage Class

The **auto** storage class is the default storage class for all local variables.

```
{
  int mount;
  auto int month;
}
```

The example above defines two variables with the same storage class, auto can only be used within functions, i.e., local variables.

The register Storage Class

The **register** storage class is used to define local variables that should be stored in a register instead of RAM. This means that the variable has a maximum size equal to the register size (usually one word) and can't have the unary '&' operator applied to it (as it does not have a memory location).

```
{
  register int miles;
}
```

The register should only be used for variables that require quick access such as counters. It should also be noted that defining 'register' does not mean that the variable will be stored in a register. It means that it MIGHT be stored in a register depending on hardware and implementation restrictions.

The static Storage Class

The **static** storage class instructs the compiler to keep a local variable in existence during the life-time of the program instead of creating and destroying it each time it comes into and goes out of scope. Therefore, making local variables static allows them to maintain their values between function calls.

The static modifier may also be applied to global variables. When this is done, it causes that variable's scope to be restricted to the file in which it is declared.

In C++, when static is used on a class data member, it causes only one copy of that member to be shared by all objects of its class.

```
#include <iostream>

// Function declaration
void func(void);

static int count = 10; /* Global variable */

main() {
  while(count--) {
    func();
  }

  return 0;
}

// Function definition
void func( void ) {
    static int i = 5; // local static variable
    i++;
```

```
std::cout << "i is " << i ;
std::cout << " and count is " << count << std::endl;
}
```

When the above code is compiled and executed, it produces the following result −

```
i is 6 and count is 9
i is 7 and count is 8
i is 8 and count is 7
i is 9 and count is 6
i is 10 and count is 5
i is 11 and count is 4
i is 12 and count is 3
i is 13 and count is 2
i is 14 and count is 1
i is 15 and count is 0
```

The extern Storage Class

The **extern** storage class is used to give a reference of a global variable that is visible to ALL the program files. When you use 'extern' the variable cannot be initialized as all it does is point the variable name at a storage location that has been previously defined.

When you have multiple files and you define a global variable or function, which will be used in other files also, then *extern* will be used in another file to give reference of defined variable or function. Just for understanding *extern* is used to declare a global variable or function in another file.

The extern modifier is most commonly used when there are two or more files sharing the same global variables or functions as explained below.

First File: main.cpp

```
#include <iostream>
int count ;
extern void write_extern();

main() {
  count = 5;
  write_extern();
}
```

Second File: support.cpp

```
#include <iostream>

extern int count;

void write_extern(void) {
  std::cout << "Count is " << count << std::endl;
}
```

Here, *extern* keyword is being used to declare count in another file. Now compile these two files as follows −

$g++ main.cpp support.cpp -o write

This will produce **write** executable program, try to execute **write** and check the result as follows −

```
$./write
5
```

The mutable Storage Class

The **mutable** specifier applies only to class objects, which are discussed later in this tutorial. It allows a member of an object to override const member function. That is, a mutable member can be modified by a const member function.

Operators in C++:

An operator is a symbol that tells the compiler to perform specific mathematical or logical manipulations. C++ is rich in built-in operators and provide the following types of operators −

- Arithmetic Operators
- Relational Operators
- Logical Operators
- Bitwise Operators
- Assignment Operators
- Misc Operators

This chapter will examine the arithmetic, relational, logical, bitwise, assignment and other operators one by one.

Arithmetic Operators

There are following arithmetic operators supported by C++ language −

Assume variable A holds 10 and variable B holds 20, then −

Operator	Description	Example
+	Adds two operands	A + B will give 30
-	Subtracts second operand from the first	A - B will give -10
*	Multiplies both operands	A * B will give 200
/	Divides numerator by de-numerator	B / A will give 2
%	Modulus Operator and remainder of after an integer division	B % A will give 0
++	Increment operator, increases integer value by one	A++ will give 11
--	Decrement operator, decreases integer	A-- will give 9

value by one

Example:

Try the following example to understand all the arithmetic operators available in C++.

Copy and paste the following C++ program in test.cpp file and compile and run this program.

```cpp
#include <iostream>
using namespace std;

main() {
  int a = 21;
  int b = 10;
  int c ;

  c = a + b;
  cout << "Line 1 - Value of c is :" << c << endl ;

  c = a - b;
  cout << "Line 2 - Value of c is :" << c << endl
;
  c = a * b;
  cout << "Line 3 - Value of c is :" << c << endl ;

  c = a / b;
  cout << "Line 4 - Value of c is :" << c << endl ;

  c = a % b;
  cout << "Line 5 - Value of c is :" << c << endl ;
```

```
c = a++;
cout << "Line 6 - Value of c is :" << c << endl ;

c = a--;
cout << "Line 7 - Value of c is  :" << c << endl ;

return 0;
}
```

When the above code is compiled and executed, it produces the following result −

```
Line 1 - Value of c is :31
Line 2 - Value of c is  :11
Line 3 - Value of c is :210
Line 4 - Value of c is  :2
Line 5 - Value of c is  :1
Line 6 - Value of c is :21
Line 7 - Value of c is  :22
```

Relational Operators:

There are following relational operators supported by C++ language

Assume variable A holds 10 and variable B holds 20, then −

Operator	Description	Example

==	Checks if the values of two operands are equal or not, if yes then condition becomes true.	(A == B) is not true.
!=	Checks if the values of two operands are equal or not, if values are not equal then condition becomes true.	(A != B) is true.
>	Checks if the value of left operand is greater than the value of right operand, if yes then condition becomes true.	(A > B) is not true.
<	Checks if the value of left operand is less than the value of right operand, if yes then condition becomes true.	(A < B) is true.

>=	Checks if the value of left operand is greater than or equal to the value of right operand, if yes then condition becomes true.	(A >= B) is not true.
<=	Checks if the value of left operand is less than or equal to the value of right operand, if yes then condition becomes true.	(A <= B) is true.

Example:

Try the following example to understand all the relational operators available in C++.

Copy and paste the following C++ program in test.cpp file and compile and run this program.

```
#include <iostream>
using namespace std;

main() {
  int a = 21;
  int b = 10;
```

```cpp
int c ;

if( a == b ) {
   cout << "Line 1 - a is equal to b" << endl ;
} else {
   cout << "Line 1 - a is not equal to b" << endl ;
}

if( a < b ) {
   cout << "Line 2 - a is less than b" << endl ;
} else {
   cout << "Line 2 - a is not less than b" << endl ;
}

if( a > b ) {
   cout << "Line 3 - a is greater than b" << endl ;
} else {
   cout << "Line 3 - a is not greater than b" << endl ;
}

/* Let's change the values of a and b */
a = 5;
b = 20;
if( a <= b ) {
   cout << "Line 4 - a is either less than \ or equal to  b"
<< endl ;
}

if( b >= a ) {
   cout << "Line 5 - b is either greater than \ or equal to b"
<< endl ;
}

return 0;
}
```

When the above code is compiled and executed, it produces the following result −

Line 1 - a is not equal to b
Line 2 - a is not less than b
Line 3 - a is greater than b
Line 4 - a is either less than or euqal to b
Line 5 - b is either greater than or equal to b

Logical Operators

There are following logical operators supported by C++ language.

Assume variable A holds 1 and variable B holds 0, then −

Operator	Description	Example
&&	Called Logical AND operator. If both the operands are non-zero, then condition becomes true.	(A && B) is false.
||	Called Logical OR Operator. If any of the two operands is non-	(A || B) is true.

	zero, then condition becomes true.	
!	Called Logical NOT Operator. Use to reverses the logical state of its operand. If a condition is true, then Logical NOT operator will make false.	!(A && B) is true.

Example:

Try the following example to understand all the logical operators available in C++.

Copy and paste the following C++ program in test.cpp file and compile and run this program.

```
#include <iostream>
using namespace std;

main() {
   int a = 5;
   int b = 20;
   int c ;

   if(a && b) {
      cout << "Line 1 - Condition is true"<< endl ;
   }
```

```
if(a || b) {
  cout << "Line 2 - Condition is true"<< endl ;
}

/* Let's change the values of a and b */
a = 0;
b = 10;

if(a && b) {
  cout << "Line 3 - Condition is true"<< endl ;
} else {
  cout << "Line 4 - Condition is not true"<< endl ;
}

if(!(a && b)) {
  cout << "Line 5 - Condition is true"<< endl ;
}

return 0;
}
```

When the above code is compiled and executed, it produces the following result −

```
Line 1 - Condition is true
Line 2 - Condition is true
Line 4 - Condition is not true
Line 5 - Condition is true
```

Bitwise Operators

Bitwise operator works on bits and perform bit-by-bit operation. The truth tables for &, |, and ^ are as follows −

p	q	p & q	p | q	p ^ q
0	0	0	0	0
0	1	0	1	1
1	1	1	1	0
1	0	0	1	1

Assume if A = 60; and B = 13; now in binary format they will be as follows −

A = 0011 1100

B = 0000 1101

A&B = 0000 1100

A|B = 0011 1101

A^B = 0011 0001

~A = 1100 0011

The Bitwise operators supported by C++ language are listed in the following table. Assume variable A holds 60 and variable B holds 13, then −

Operator	Description	Example
&	Binary AND Operator copies a bit to the result if it exists in both operands.	(A & B) will give 12 which is 0000 1100
|	Binary OR Operator copies a bit if it exists in either operand.	(A | B) will give 61 which is 0011 1101
^	Binary XOR Operator copies the bit if it is set in one operand but not both.	(A ^ B) will give 49 which is 0011 0001
~	Binary Ones Complement Operator is unary and has the effect of 'flipping' bits.	(~A) will give -61 which is 1100 0011 in 2's complement form due to a signed binary number.
<<	Binary Left Shift Operator. The left operands value is moved left by the	A << 2 will give 240 which is 1111 0000

	number of bits specified by the right operand.	
>>	Binary Right Shift Operator. The left operands value is moved right by the number of bits specified by the right operand.	A >> 2 will give 15 which is 0000 1111

Example:

Try the following example to understand all the bitwise operators available in C++.

Copy and paste the following C++ program in test.cpp file and compile and run this program.

```
#include <iostream>
using namespace std;

main() {
    unsigned int a = 60;        // 60 = 0011 1100
    unsigned int b = 13;        // 13 = 0000 1101
    int c = 0;

    c = a & b;          // 12 = 0000 1100
    cout << "Line 1 - Value of c is : " << c << endl ;
```

```
c = a | b;        // 61 = 0011 1101
cout << "Line 2 - Value of c is: " << c << endl ;

c = a ^ b;        // 49 = 0011 0001
cout << "Line 3 - Value of c is: " << c << endl ;

c = ~a;           // -61 = 1100 0011
cout << "Line 4 - Value of c is: " << c << endl ;

c = a << 2;       // 240 = 1111 0000
cout << "Line 5 - Value of c is: " << c << endl ;

c = a >> 2;       // 15 = 0000 1111
cout << "Line 6 - Value of c is: " << c << endl ;

return 0;
}
```

When the above code is compiled and executed, it produces the following result −

```
Line 1 - Value of c is : 12
Line 2 - Value of c is: 61
Line 3 - Value of c is: 49
Line 4 - Value of c is: -61
Line 5 - Value of c is: 240
Line 6 - Value of c is: 15
```

Assignment Operators

There are following assignment operators supported by C++ language −

Operator	Description	Example
=	Simple assignment operator, Assigns values from right side operands to left side operand.	C = A + B will assign value of A + B into C
+=	Add AND assignment operator, It adds right operand to the left operand and assign the result to left operand.	C += A is equivalent to C = C + A
-=	Subtract AND assignment operator, It subtracts right operand from the left operand and assign the result to left operand.	C -= A is equivalent to C = C - A

*=	Multiply AND assignment operator, It multiplies right operand with the left operand and assign the result to left operand.	C *= A is equivalent to C = C * A
/=	Divide AND assignment operator, It divides left operand with the right operand and assign the result to left operand.	C /= A is equivalent to C = C / A
%=	Modulus AND assignment operator, It takes modulus using two operands and assign the result to left operand.	C %= A is equivalent to C = C % A
<<=	Left shift AND assignment operator.	C <<= 2 is same as C = C << 2
>>=	Right shift AND assignment operator.	C >>= 2 is same as C = C >> 2

&=	Bitwise AND assignment operator.	C &= 2 is same as C = C & 2
^=	Bitwise exclusive OR and assignment operator.	C ^= 2 is same as C = C ^ 2
|=	Bitwise inclusive OR and assignment operator.	C |= 2 is same as C = C | 2

Example:

Try the following example to understand all the assignment operators available in C++.

Copy and paste the following C++ program in test.cpp file and compile and run this program.

```
#include <iostream>
using namespace std;

main() {
  int a = 21;
  int c ;

  c = a;
  cout << "Line 1 - = Operator, Value of c = : " <<c<<
endl ;
```

```
c += a;
cout << "Line 2 - += Operator, Value of c = : " <<c<<
endl ;

c -= a;
cout << "Line 3 - -= Operator, Value of c = : " <<c<<
endl ;

c *= a;
cout << "Line 4 - *= Operator, Value of c = : " <<c<<
endl ;

c /= a;
cout << "Line 5 - /= Operator, Value of c = : " <<c<<
endl ;

c = 200;
c %= a;
cout << "Line 6 - %= Operator, Value of c = : " <<c<<
endl ;

c <<= 2;
cout << "Line 7 - <<= Operator, Value of c = : " <<c<<
endl ;

c >>= 2;
cout << "Line 8 - >>= Operator, Value of c = : " <<c<<
endl ;

c &= 2;
cout << "Line 9 - &= Operator, Value of c = : " <<c<<
endl ;

c ^= 2;
```

```
cout << "Line 10 - ^= Operator, Value of c = : " <<c<<
endl ;

c |= 2;
cout << "Line 11 - |= Operator, Value of c = : " <<c<<
endl ;

return 0;
}
```

When the above code is compiled and executed, it produces the following result −

```
Line 1 - = Operator, Value of c = : 21
Line 2 - += Operator, Value of c = : 42
Line 3 - -= Operator, Value of c = : 21
Line 4 - *= Operator, Value of c = : 441
Line 5 - /= Operator, Value of c = : 21
Line 6 - %= Operator, Value of c = : 11
Line 7 - <<= Operator, Value of c = : 44
Line 8 - >>= Operator, Value of c = : 11
Line 9 - &= Operator, Value of c = : 2
Line 10 - ^= Operator, Value of c = : 0
Line 11 - |= Operator, Value of c = : 2
```

Misc Operators:

The following table lists some other operators that C++ supports.

Sr.No	Operator & Description
1	**sizeof** sizeof operator returns the size of a variable. For example, sizeof(a), where 'a' is integer, and will return 4.
2	**Condition ? X : Y** Conditional operator (?). If Condition is true then it returns value of X otherwise returns value of Y.
3	**,** Comma operator causes a sequence of operations to be performed. The value of the entire comma expression is the value of the last expression of the comma-separated list.
4	**. (dot) and -> (arrow)** Member operators are used to reference individual members of classes, structures, and unions.

5	**Cast**
	Casting operators convert one data type to another. For example, int(2.2000) would return 2.
6	**&**
	Pointer operator & returns the address of a variable. For example &a; will give actual address of the variable.
7	*
	Pointer operator * is pointer to a variable. For example *var; will pointer to a variable var.

Example:

Sizeof operator:

The **sizeof** is a keyword, but it is a compile-time operator that determines the size, in bytes, of a variable or data type.

The sizeof operator can be used to get the size of classes, structures, unions and any other user defined data type.

The syntax of using sizeof is as follows −

sizeof (data type)

Where data type is the desired data type including classes, structures, unions and any other user defined data type.

Try the following example to understand all the sizeof operator available in C++. Copy and paste following C++ program in test.cpp file and compile and run this program.

```cpp
#include <iostream>
using namespace std;

int main() {
  cout << "Size of char : " << sizeof(char) << endl;
  cout << "Size of int : " << sizeof(int) << endl;
  cout << "Size of short int : " << sizeof(short int) << endl;
  cout << "Size of long int : " << sizeof(long int) << endl;
  cout << "Size of float : " << sizeof(float) << endl;
  cout << "Size of double : " << sizeof(double) << endl;
  cout << "Size of wchar_t : " << sizeof(wchar_t) << endl;

  return 0;
}
```

When the above code is compiled and executed, it produces the following result, which can vary from machine to machine −

```
Size of char : 1
Size of int : 4
Size of short int : 2
Size of long int : 4
Size of float : 4
Size of double : 8
Size of wchar_t : 4
```

Conditional operator:

Exp1 ? Exp2 : Exp3;

where Exp1, Exp2, and Exp3 are expressions. Notice the use and placement of the colon. The value of a ? expression is determined like this: Exp1 is evaluated. If it is true, then Exp2 is evaluated and becomes the value of the entire ? expression. If Exp1 is false, then Exp3 is evaluated and its value becomes the value of the expression.

The ? is called a ternary operator because it requires three operands and can be used to replace if-else statements, which have the following form −

```
if(condition) {
   var = X;
} else {
   var = Y;
}
```

For example, consider the following code −

```
if(y < 10) {
   var = 30;
} else {
   var = 40;
}
```

Above code can be rewritten like this −

```
var = (y < 10) ? 30 : 40;
```

Here, x is assigned the value of 30 if y is less than 10 and 40 if it is not.

You can try the following example −

```
#include <iostream>
using namespace std;

int main () {
   // Local variable declaration:
   int x, y = 10;

   x = (y < 10) ? 30 : 40;
   cout << "value of x: " << x << endl;

   return 0;
}
```

When the above code is compiled and executed, it produces the following result −

value of x: 40

Comma Operator:

The purpose of comma operator is to string together several expressions. The value of a comma-separated list of expressions is the value of the right-most expression. Essentially, the comma's effect is to cause a sequence of operations to be performed.

The values of the other expressions will be discarded. This means that the expression on the right side will become the value of the entire comma-separated expression.

For example −

var = (count = 19, incr = 10, count+1);

Here first assigns count the value 19, assigns incr the value 10, then adds 1 to count, and finally, assigns var the value of the rightmost expression, count+1, which is 20. The parentheses are necessary because the comma operator has a lower precedence than the assignment operator.

To see the effects of the comma operator, try running the following program –

```cpp
#include <iostream>
using namespace std;

int main() {
    int i, j;

    j = 10;
    i = (j++, j+100, 999+j);

    cout << i;

    return 0;
}
```

When the above code is compiled and executed, it produces the following result –

1010

Here is the procedure how the value of i gets calculated: j starts with the value 10. j is then incremented to 11. Next, j is added to 100. Finally, j (still containing 11) is added to 999, which yields the result 1010.

Operators Precedence in C++

Operator precedence determines the grouping of terms in an expression. This affects how an expression is evaluated. Certain operators have higher precedence than others; for example, the multiplication operator has higher precedence than the addition operator –

For example x = 7 + 3 * 2; here, x is assigned 13, not 20 because operator * has higher precedence than +, so it first gets multiplied with 3*2 and then adds into 7.

Here, operators with the highest precedence appear at the top of the table, those with the lowest appear at the bottom. Within an expression, higher precedence operators will be evaluated first.

Category	Operator	Associativity
Postfix	() [] -> . ++ - -	Left to right
Unary	+ - ! ~ ++ - - (type)* & sizeof	Right to left
Multiplicative	* / %	Left to right
Additive	+ -	Left to right

Shift	<< >>	Left to right
Relational	< <= > >=	Left to right
Equality	== !=	Left to right
Bitwise AND	&	Left to right
Bitwise XOR	^	Left to right
Bitwise OR	|	Left to right
Logical AND	&&	Left to right
Logical OR	||	Left to right
Conditional	?:	Right to left
Assignment	= += -= *= /= %=>>= <<= &= ^= |=	Right to left

Comma	,	Left to right

Example:

Try the following example to understand operators precedence concept available in C++. Copy and paste the following C++ program in test.cpp file and compile and run this program.

Check the simple difference with and without parenthesis. This will produce different results because (), /, * and + have different precedence.

Higher precedence operators will be evaluated first −

```cpp
#include <iostream>
using namespace std;

main() {
    int a = 20;
    int b = 10;
    int c = 15;
    int d = 5;
    int e;

    e = (a + b) * c / d;    // ( 30 * 15 ) / 5
    cout << "Value of (a + b) * c / d is :" << e << endl ;

    e = ((a + b) * c) / d;   // (30 * 15 ) / 5
    cout << "Value of ((a + b) * c) / d is :" << e << endl ;

    e = (a + b) * (c / d);   // (30) * (15/5)
    cout << "Value of (a + b) * (c / d) is :" << e << endl ;
```

```
e = a + (b * c) / d;    // 20 + (150/5)
cout << "Value of a + (b * c) / d is :" << e << endl ;

return 0;
}
```

When the above code is compiled and executed, it produces the following result −

```
Value of (a + b) * c / d is :90
Value of ((a + b) * c) / d is :90
Value of (a + b) * (c / d) is :90
Value of a + (b * c) / d is :50
```

C++ Loop Types

There may be a situation, when you need to execute a block of code several number of times. In general, statements are executed sequentially: The first statement in a function is executed first, followed by the second, and so on.

Programming languages provide various control structures that allow for more complicated execution paths.

A loop statement allows us to execute a statement or group of statements multiple times and following is the general from of a loop statement in most of the programming languages –

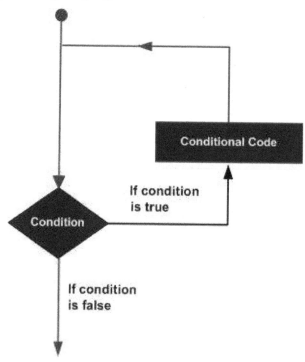

C++ programming language provides the following type of loops to handle looping requirements.

Sr.No	Loop Type & Description
1	while loop Repeats a statement or group of statements while a given condition is true. It tests the condition before executing the loop body.
2	for loop Execute a sequence of statements multiple times and abbreviates the code that manages the loop variable.
3	do...while loop Like a 'while' statement, except that it tests the condition at the end of the loop body.
4	nested loops You can use one or more loop inside any another 'while', 'for' or 'do..while' loop.

While loop:

A **while** loop statement repeatedly executes a target statement as long as a given condition is true.

Syntax

The syntax of a while loop in C++ is −

```
while(condition) {
    statement(s);
}
```

Here, **statement(s)** may be a single statement or a block of statements. The **condition** may be any expression, and true is any non-zero value. The loop iterates while the condition is true.

When the condition becomes false, program control passes to the line immediately following the loop.

Flow Diagram

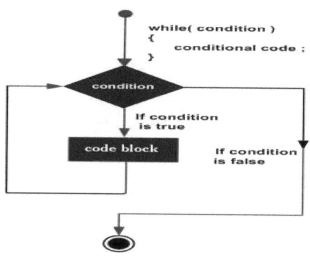

Here, key point of the *while* loop is that the loop might not ever run. When the condition is tested and the result is false, the loop body will be skipped and the first statement after the while loop will be executed.

Example

```
#include <iostream>
using namespace std;

int main () {
   // Local variable declaration:
   int a = 10;

   // while loop execution
   while( a < 20 ) {
      cout << "value of a: " << a << endl;
      a++;
   }

   return 0;
}
```

When the above code is compiled and executed, it produces the following result −

```
value of a: 10
value of a: 11
value of a: 12
value of a: 13
value of a: 14
value of a: 15
value of a: 16
value of a: 17
value of a: 18
value of a: 19
```

For loop:

A **for** loop is a repetition control structure that allows you to efficiently write a loop that needs to execute a specific number of times.

Syntax

The syntax of a for loop in C++ is −

```
for ( init; condition; increment ) {
    statement(s);
}
```

Here is the flow of control in a for loop −

- The **init** step is executed first, and only once. This step allows you to declare and initialize any loop control variables. You are not required to put a statement here, as long as a semicolon appears.

- Next, the **condition** is evaluated. If it is true, the body of the loop is executed. If it is false, the body of the loop does not execute and flow of control jumps to the next statement just after the for loop.

- After the body of the for loop executes, the flow of control jumps back up to the **increment** statement. This statement can be left blank, as long as a semicolon appears after the condition.

- The condition is now evaluated again. If it is true, the loop executes and the process repeats itself (body of loop, then increment step, and then again condition). After the condition becomes false, the for loop terminates.

Flow Diagram

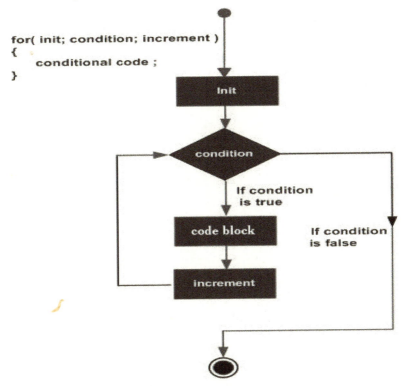

```
for( init; condition; increment )
{
    conditional code ;
}
```

Example

```cpp
#include <iostream>
using namespace std;

int main () {
   // for loop execution
   for( int a = 10; a < 20; a = a + 1 ) {
      cout << "value of a: " << a << endl;
   }
```

```
   return 0;
}
```

When the above code is compiled and executed, it produces the following result –

```
value of a: 10
value of a: 11
value of a: 12
value of a: 13
value of a: 14
value of a: 15
value of a: 16
value of a: 17
value of a: 18
value of a: 19
```

do...while loop:

Unlike **for** and **while** loops, which test the loop condition at the top of the loop, the **do...while** loop checks its condition at the bottom of the loop.

A **do...while** loop is similar to a while loop, except that a do...while loop is guaranteed to execute at least one time.

Syntax

The syntax of a do...while loop in C++ is –

```
do {
   statement(s);
}
while( condition );
```

Notice that the conditional expression appears at the end of the loop, so the statement(s) in the loop execute once before the condition is tested.

If the condition is true, the flow of control jumps back up to do, and the statement(s) in the loop execute again. This process repeats until the given condition becomes false.

Flow Diagram

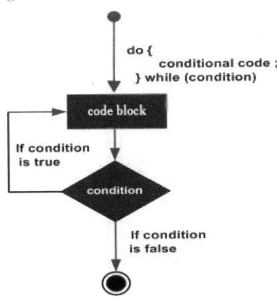

Example

```
#include <iostream>
using namespace std;

int main () {
    // Local variable declaration:
    int a = 10;
```

```
// do loop execution
do {
   cout << "value of a: " << a << endl;
   a = a + 1;
} while( a < 20 );

return 0;
}
```

When the above code is compiled and executed, it produces the following result –

```
value of a: 10
value of a: 11
value of a: 12
value of a: 13
value of a: 14
value of a: 15
value of a: 16
value of a: 17
value of a: 18
value of a: 19
```

Nested loops:

A loop can be nested inside of another loop. C++ allows at least 256 levels of nesting.

Syntax

The syntax for a **nested for loop** statement in C++ is as follows –

```
for ( init; condition; increment ) {
   for ( init; condition; increment ) {
```

```
      statement(s);
    }
  statement(s); // you can put more statements.
}
```

The syntax for a **nested while loop** statement in C++ is as follows −

```
while(condition) {
  while(condition) {
    statement(s);
  }
  statement(s); // you can put more statements.
}
```

The syntax for a **nested do...while loop** statement in C++ is as follows −

```
do {
  statement(s); // you can put more statements.
  do {
    statement(s);
  } while( condition );

} while( condition );
```

Example

The following program uses a nested for loop to find the prime numbers from 2 to 100 −

```
#include <iostream>
using namespace std;

int main () {
  int i, j;
```

```
for(i = 2; i<100; i++) {
   for(j = 2; j <= (i/j); j++)
   if(!(i%j)) break; // if factor found, not prime
   if(j > (i/j)) cout << i << " is prime\n";
}

return 0;
}
```

This would produce the following result −

```
2 is prime
3 is prime
5 is prime
7 is prime
11 is prime
13 is prime
17 is prime
19 is prime
23 is prime
29 is prime
31 is prime
37 is prime
41 is prime
43 is prime
47 is prime
53 is prime
59 is prime
61 is prime
67 is prime
71 is prime
73 is prime
79 is prime
83 is prime
89 is prime
97 is prime
```

Loop Control Statements:

Loop control statements change execution from its normal sequence. When execution leaves a scope, all automatic objects that were created in that scope are destroyed.

C++ supports the following control statements.

Sr.No	Control Statement & Description
1	break statement Terminates the **loop** or **switch** statement and transfers execution to the statement immediately following the loop or switch.
2	continue statement Causes the loop to skip the remainder of its body and immediately retest its condition prior to reiterating.
3	goto statement Transfers control to the labeled statement. Though it is not advised to use goto statement in your program.

Break statement:

The **break** statement has the following two usages in C++ –

- When the **break** statement is encountered inside a loop, the loop is immediately terminated and program control resumes at the next statement following the loop.

- It can be used to terminate a case in the **switch** statement (covered in the next chapter).

If you are using nested loops (i.e., one loop inside another loop), the break statement will stop the execution of the innermost loop and start executing the next line of code after the block.

Syntax:

The syntax of a break statement in C++ is –

```
break;
```

Flow Diagram

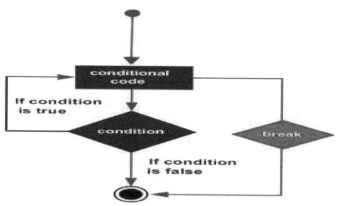

Example

```cpp
#include <iostream>
using namespace std;

int main () {
   // Local variable declaration:
   int a = 10;

   // do loop execution
   do {
      cout << "value of a: " << a << endl;
      a = a + 1;
      if( a > 15) {
         // terminate the loop
         break;
      }
   } while( a < 20 );

   return 0;
}
```

When the above code is compiled and executed, it produces the following result –

```
value of a: 10
value of a: 11
value of a: 12
value of a: 13
value of a: 14
value of a: 15
```

Continue statement:

The **continue** statement works somewhat like the break statement. Instead of forcing termination, however, continue forces the next iteration of the loop to take place, skipping any code in between.

For the **for** loop, continue causes the conditional test and increment portions of the loop to execute. For the **while** and **do...while** loops, program control passes to the conditional tests.

Syntax

The syntax of a continue statement in C++ is −

```
continue;
```

Flow Diagram

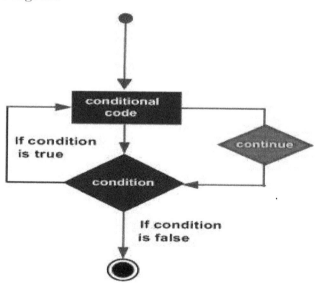

Example

```
#include <iostream>
using namespace std;

int main () {
   // Local variable declaration:
   int a = 10;

   // do loop execution
   do {
      if( a == 15) {
         // skip the iteration.
         a = a + 1;
         continue;
      }
      cout << "value of a: " << a << endl;
      a = a + 1;
   }
   while( a < 20 );

   return 0;
}
```

When the above code is compiled and executed, it produces the following result −

```
value of a: 10
value of a: 11
value of a: 12
value of a: 13
value of a: 14
value of a: 16
value of a: 17
value of a: 18
value of a: 19
```

The Infinite Loop

A loop becomes infinite loop if a condition never becomes false. The **for** loop is traditionally used for this purpose. Since none of the three expressions that form the 'for' loop are required, you can make an endless loop by leaving the conditional expression empty.

```
#include <iostream>
using namespace std;

int main () {
  for( ; ; ) {
    printf("This loop will run forever.\n");
  }

  return 0;
}
```

When the conditional expression is absent, it is assumed to be true. You may have an initialization and increment expression, but C++ programmers more commonly use the 'for (;;)' construct to signify an infinite loop.

NOTE – You can terminate an infinite loop by pressing Ctrl + C keys.

C++ decision making statements

Decision making structures require that the programmer specify one or more conditions to be evaluated or tested by the program, along with a statement or statements to be executed if the condition is determined to be true, and optionally, other statements to be executed if the condition is determined to be false.

Following is the general form of a typical decision making structure found in most of the programming languages −

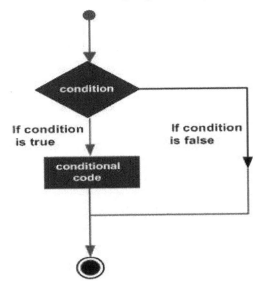

C++ programming language provides following types of decision making statements.

Sr.No	Statement & Description

1	if statement An 'if' statement consists of a boolean expression followed by one or more statements.
2	if...else statement An 'if' statement can be followed by an optional 'else' statement, which executes when the boolean expression is false.
3	switch statement A 'switch' statement allows a variable to be tested for equality against a list of values.
4	nested if statements You can use one 'if' or 'else if' statement inside another 'if' or 'else if' statement(s).
5	nested switch statements You can use one 'switch' statement inside another 'switch' statement(s).

If statement:

An **if** statement consists of a boolean expression followed by one or more statements.

Syntax

The syntax of an if statement in C++ is −

```
if(boolean_expression) {
   // statement(s) will execute if the boolean expression is
true
}
```

If the boolean expression evaluates to **true**, then the block of code inside the if statement will be executed. If boolean expression evaluates to **false**, then the first set of code after the end of the if statement (after the closing curly brace) will be executed.

Flow Diagram

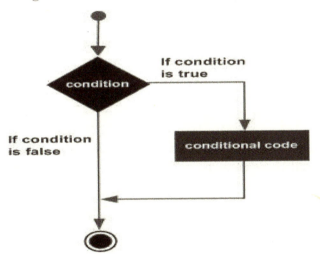

Example

```
#include <iostream>
using namespace std;
```

```
int main () {
   // local variable declaration:
   int a = 10;

   // check the boolean condition
   if( a < 20 ) {
      // if condition is true then print the following
      cout << "a is less than 20;" << endl;
   }
   cout << "value of a is : " << a << endl;

   return 0;
}
```

When the above code is compiled and executed, it produces the following result −

```
a is less than 20;
value of a is : 10
```

If...else statement:

An **if** statement can be followed by an optional **else** statement, which executes when the boolean expression is false.

Syntax:

The syntax of an if...else statement in C++ is −

```
if(boolean_expression) {
   // statement(s) will execute if the boolean expression is
true
```

```
} else {
   // statement(s) will execute if the boolean expression is
false
}
```

If the boolean expression evaluates to **true**, then the **if block** of code will be executed, otherwise **else block** of code will be executed.

Flow Diagram

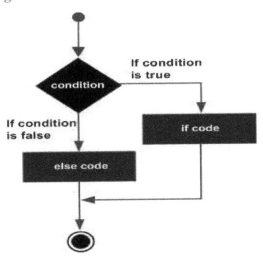

Example

```
#include <iostream>
using namespace std;

int main () {
   // local variable declaration:
   int a = 100;
```

```
// check the boolean condition
if( a < 20 ) {
    // if condition is true then print the following
    cout << "a is less than 20;" << endl;
} else {
    // if condition is false then print the following
    cout << "a is not less than 20;" << endl;
}
cout << "value of a is : " << a << endl;

return 0;
}
```

When the above code is compiled and executed, it produces the following result −

```
a is not less than 20;
value of a is : 100
```

Switch statement:

A **switch** statement allows a variable to be tested for equality against a list of values. Each value is called a case, and the variable being switched on is checked for each case.

Syntax

The syntax for a **switch** statement in C++ is as follows −

```
switch(expression) {
  case constant-expression :
     statement(s);
     break; //optional
```

```
case constant-expression :
  statement(s);
  break; //optional

// you can have any number of case statements.
default : //Optional
  statement(s);
}
```

The following rules apply to a switch statement –

- The **expression** used in a **switch** statement must have an integral or enumerated type, or be of a class type in which the class has a single conversion function to an integral or enumerated type.

- You can have any number of case statements within a switch. Each case is followed by the value to be compared to and a colon.

- The **constant-expression** for a case must be the same data type as the variable in the switch, and it must be a constant or a literal.

- When the variable being switched on is equal to a case, the statements following that case will execute until a **break** statement is reached.

- When a break statement is reached, the switch terminates, and the flow of control jumps to the next line following the switch statement.

- Not every case needs to contain a break. If no break appears, the flow of control will *fall through* to subsequent cases until a break is reached.

- A **switch** statement can have an optional **default** case, which must appear at the end of the switch. The default case can be used for performing a task when none of the cases is true. No break is needed in the default case.

Flow Diagram

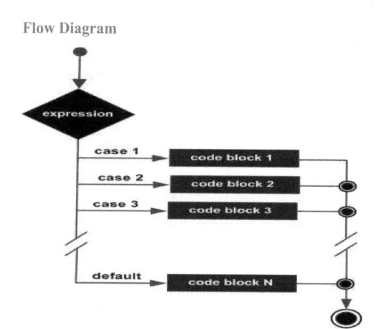

Example

```
#include <iostream>
using namespace std;

int main () {
 // local variable declaration:
 char grade = 'D';

 switch(grade) {
   case 'A' :
     cout << "Excellent!" << endl;
```

```
      break;
   case 'B' :
   case 'C' :
      cout << "Well done" << endl;
      break;
   case 'D' :
      cout << "You passed" << endl;
      break;
   case 'F' :
      cout << "Better try again" << endl;
      break;
   default :
      cout << "Invalid grade" << endl;
   }
   cout << "Your grade is " << grade << endl;

   return 0;
}
```

This would produce the following result −

```
You passed
Your grade is D
```

The ? : Operator

We have covered conditional operator "? :" in previous chapter which can be used to replace **if...else** statements. It has the following general form −

Exp1 ? Exp2 : Exp3;

Exp1, Exp2, and Exp3 are expressions. Notice the use and placement of the colon.

The value of a '?' expression is determined like this: Exp1 is evaluated. If it is true, then Exp2 is evaluated and becomes the value of the entire '?' expression. If Exp1 is false, then Exp3 is evaluated and its value becomes the value of the expression.

C++ Functions

A function is a group of statements that together perform a task. Every C++ program has at least one function, which is **main()**, and all the most trivial programs can define additional functions.

You can divide up your code into separate functions. How you divide up your code among different functions is up to you, but logically the division usually is such that each function performs a specific task.

A function **declaration** tells the compiler about a function's name, return type, and parameters. A function **definition** provides the actual body of the function.

The C++ standard library provides numerous built-in functions that your program can call. For example, function **strcat()** to concatenate two strings, function **memcpy()** to copy one memory location to another location and many more functions.

A function is known with various names like a method or a sub-routine or a procedure etc.

Defining a Function

The general form of a C++ function definition is as follows −

```
return_type function_name( parameter list ) {
    body of the function
}
```

A C++ function definition consists of a function header and a function body. Here are all the parts of a function −

- **Return Type** – A function may return a value. The **return_type** is the data type of the value the function returns. Some functions perform the desired operations without returning a value. In this case, the return_type is the keyword **void**.

- **Function Name** – This is the actual name of the function. The function name and the parameter list together constitute the function signature.

- **Parameters** – A parameter is like a placeholder. When a function is invoked, you pass a value to the parameter. This value is referred to as actual parameter or argument. The parameter list refers to the type, order, and number of the parameters of a function. Parameters are optional; that is, a function may contain no parameters.

- **Function Body** – The function body contains a collection of statements that define what the function does.

Example

Following is the source code for a function called **max()**. This function takes two parameters num1 and num2 and return the biggest of both –

// function returning the max between two numbers

```
int max(int num1, int num2) {
  // local variable declaration
  int result;

  if (num1 > num2)
    result = num1;
```

```
  else
    result = num2;

  return result;
}
```

Function Declarations

A function **declaration** tells the compiler about a function name and how to call the function. The actual body of the function can be defined separately.

A function declaration has the following parts −

```
return_type function_name( parameter list );
```

For the above defined function max(), following is the function declaration −

```
int max(int num1, int num2);
```

Parameter names are not important in function declaration only their type is required, so following is also valid declaration −

```
int max(int, int);
```

Function declaration is required when you define a function in one source file and you call that function in another file. In such case, you should declare the function at the top of the file calling the function.

Calling a Function

While creating a C++ function, you give a definition of what the function has to do. To use a function, you will have to call or invoke that function.

When a program calls a function, program control is transferred to the called function. A called function performs defined task and when it's return statement is executed or when its function-ending closing brace is reached, it returns program control back to the main program.

To call a function, you simply need to pass the required parameters along with function name, and if function returns a value, then you can store returned value. For example −

```cpp
#include <iostream>
using namespace std;

// function declaration
int max(int num1, int num2);

int main () {
   // local variable declaration:
   int a = 100;
   int b = 200;
   int ret;

   // calling a function to get max value.
   ret = max(a, b);
   cout << "Max value is : " << ret << endl;

   return 0;
}

// function returning the max between two numbers
int max(int num1, int num2) {
   // local variable declaration
   int result;
```

```
if (num1 > num2)
    result = num1;
else
    result = num2;

return result;
}
```

I kept max() function along with main() function and compiled the source code. While running final executable, it would produce the following result –

Max value is : 200

Function Arguments

If a function is to use arguments, it must declare variables that accept the values of the arguments. These variables are called the **formal parameters** of the function.

The formal parameters behave like other local variables inside the function and are created upon entry into the function and destroyed upon exit.

While calling a function, there are two ways that arguments can be passed to a function –

Sr.No	Call Type & Description
1	Call by Value This method copies the actual value of an argument into the formal parameter of the function. In this case, changes made to the parameter inside the function have no effect on

	the argument.
2	Call by Pointer This method copies the address of an argument into the formal parameter. Inside the function, the address is used to access the actual argument used in the call. This means that changes made to the parameter affect the argument.
3	Call by Reference This method copies the reference of an argument into the formal parameter. Inside the function, the reference is used to access the actual argument used in the call. This means that changes made to the parameter affect the argument.

By default, C++ uses **call by value** to pass arguments. In general, this means that code within a function cannot alter the arguments used to call the function and above mentioned example while calling max() function used the same method.

Call by Value:

The **call by value** method of passing arguments to a function copies the actual value of an argument into the formal parameter of the function. In this case, changes made to the parameter inside the function have no effect on the argument.

By default, C++ uses call by value to pass arguments. In general, this means that code within a function cannot alter the arguments used to call the function. Consider the function **swap()** definition as follows.

```
// function definition to swap the values.
void swap(int x, int y) {
  int temp;

  temp = x; /* save the value of x */
  x = y;   /* put y into x */
  y = temp; /* put x into y */

  return;
}
```

Now, let us call the function **swap()** by passing actual values as in the following example −

```
#include <iostream>
using namespace std;

// function declaration
void swap(int x, int y);

int main () {
  // local variable declaration:
  int a = 100;
  int b = 200;

  cout << "Before swap, value of a :" << a << endl;
  cout << "Before swap, value of b :" << b << endl;

  // calling a function to swap the values.
  swap(a, b);
```

```
cout << "After swap, value of a :" << a << endl;
cout << "After swap, value of b :" << b << endl;

return 0;
}
```

When the above code is put together in a file, compiled and executed, it produces the following result −

```
Before swap, value of a :100
Before swap, value of b :200
After swap, value of a :100
After swap, value of b :200
```

Which shows that there is no change in the values though they had been changed inside the function.

Call by Pointer:

The **call by pointer** method of passing arguments to a function copies the address of an argument into the formal parameter. Inside the function, the address is used to access the actual argument used in the call. This means that changes made to the parameter affect the passed argument.

To pass the value by pointer, argument pointers are passed to the functions just like any other value. So accordingly you need to declare the function parameters as pointer types as in the following function **swap()**, which exchanges the values of the two integer variables pointed to by its arguments.

```
// function definition to swap the values.
void swap(int *x, int *y) {
```

```
int temp;
temp = *x; /* save the value at address x */
*x = *y; /* put y into x */
*y = temp; /* put x into y */

return;
}
```

To check the more detail about C++ pointers, kindly check C++ Pointers chapter.

For now, let us call the function **swap()** by passing values by pointer as in the following example −

```
#include <iostream>
using namespace std;

// function declaration
void swap(int *x, int *y);

int main () {
   // local variable declaration:
   int a = 100;
   int b = 200;

   cout << "Before swap, value of a :" << a << endl;
   cout << "Before swap, value of b :" << b << endl;

   /* calling a function to swap the values.
    * &a indicates pointer to a ie. address of variable a and
    * &b indicates pointer to b ie. address of variable b.
    */
   swap(&a, &b);

   cout << "After swap, value of a :" << a << endl;
   cout << "After swap, value of b :" << b << endl;
```

```
   return 0;
}
```

When the above code is put together in a file, compiled and executed, it produces the following result −

```
Before swap, value of a :100
Before swap, value of b :200
After swap, value of a :200
After swap, value of b :100
```

Call by Reference:

The **call by reference** method of passing arguments to a function copies the reference of an argument into the formal parameter. Inside the function, the reference is used to access the actual argument used in the call. This means that changes made to the parameter affect the passed argument.

To pass the value by reference, argument reference is passed to the functions just like any other value. So accordingly you need to declare the function parameters as reference types as in the following function **swap()**, which exchanges the values of the two integer variables pointed to by its arguments.

```
// function definition to swap the values.
void swap(int &x, int &y) {
   int temp;
   temp = x; /* save the value at address x */
   x = y;    /* put y into x */
   y = temp; /* put x into y */
```

```
return;
}
```

For now, let us call the function **swap()** by passing values by reference as in the following example −

```cpp
#include <iostream>
using namespace std;

// function declaration
void swap(int &x, int &y);

int main () {
   // local variable declaration:
   int a = 100;
   int b = 200;

   cout << "Before swap, value of a :" << a << endl;
   cout << "Before swap, value of b :" << b << endl;

   /* calling a function to swap the values using variable
   reference.*/
   swap(a, b);

   cout << "After swap, value of a :" << a << endl;
   cout << "After swap, value of b :" << b << endl;

   return 0;
}
```

When the above code is put together in a file, compiled and executed, it produces the following result −

```
Before swap, value of a :100
Before swap, value of b :200
After swap, value of a :200
```

After swap, value of b :100

Default Values for Parameters

When you define a function, you can specify a default value for each of the last parameters. This value will be used if the corresponding argument is left blank when calling to the function.

This is done by using the assignment operator and assigning values for the arguments in the function definition. If a value for that parameter is not passed when the function is called, the default given value is used, but if a value is specified, this default value is ignored and the passed value is used instead. Consider the following example –

```cpp
#include <iostream>
using namespace std;

int sum(int a, int b = 20) {
   int result;
   result = a + b;

   return (result);
}
int main () {
   // local variable declaration:
   int a = 100;
   int b = 200;
   int result;

   // calling a function to add the values.
   result = sum(a, b);
   cout << "Total value is :" << result << endl;
```

```
// calling a function again as follows.
result = sum(a);
cout << "Total value is :" << result << endl;

return 0;
}
```

When the above code is compiled and executed, it produces the following result −

```
Total value is :300
Total value is :120
```

Numbers in C++

Normally, when we work with Numbers, we use primitive data types such as int, short, long, float and double, etc. The number data types, their possible values and number ranges have been explained while discussing C++ Data Types.

Defining Numbers in C++

You have already defined numbers in various examples given in previous chapters. Here is another consolidated example to define various types of numbers in C++ −

```cpp
#include <iostream>
using namespace std;

int main () {
   // number definition:
   short  s;
   int    i;
   long   l;
   float  f;
   double d;

   // number assignments;
   s = 10;
   i = 1000;
   l = 1000000;
   f = 230.47;
   d = 30949.374;

   // number printing;
   cout << "short  s :" << s << endl;
   cout << "int    i :" << i << endl;
```

```
cout << "long  1 :" << l << endl;
cout << "float  f :" << f << endl;
cout << "double d :" << d << endl;

return 0;
}
```

When the above code is compiled and executed, it produces the following result –

```
short  s :10
int    i :1000
long   l :1000000
float  f :230.47
double d :30949.4
```

Math Operations in C++

In addition to the various functions you can create, C++ also includes some useful functions you can use. These functions are available in standard C and C++ libraries and called **built-in** functions. These are functions that can be included in your program and then use.

C++ has a rich set of mathematical operations, which can be performed on various numbers. Following table lists down some useful built-in mathematical functions available in C++.

To utilize these functions you need to include the math header file **<cmath>**.

Sr.No	Function & Purpose

1	**double cos(double);** This function takes an angle (as a double) and returns the cosine.
2	**double sin(double);** This function takes an angle (as a double) and returns the sine.
3	**double tan(double);** This function takes an angle (as a double) and returns the tangent.
4	**double log(double);** This function takes a number and returns the natural log of that number.
5	**double pow(double, double);** The first is a number you wish to raise and the second is the power you wish to raise it t
6	**double hypot(double, double);** If you pass this function the length of two sides of a right triangle, it will return you the length of the hypotenuse.

7	**double sqrt(double);**
	You pass this function a number and it gives you the square root.
8	**int abs(int);**
	This function returns the absolute value of an integer that is passed to it.
9	**double fabs(double);**
	This function returns the absolute value of any decimal number passed to it.
10	**double floor(double);**
	Finds the integer which is less than or equal to the argument passed to it.

Following is a simple example to show few of the mathematical operations −

```cpp
#include <iostream>
#include <cmath>
using namespace std;

int main () {
   // number definition:
   short s = 10;
   int   i = -1000;
   long  l = 100000;
```

```
float  f = 230.47;
double d = 200.374;

// mathematical operations;
cout << "sin(d) :" << sin(d) << endl;
cout << "abs(i) :" << abs(i) << endl;
cout << "floor(d) :" << floor(d) << endl;
cout << "sqrt(f) :" << sqrt(f) << endl;
cout << "pow( d, 2) :" << pow(d, 2) << endl;

return 0;
}
```

When the above code is compiled and executed, it produces the following result −

```
sign(d)    :-0.634939
abs(i)     :1000
floor(d)   :200
sqrt(f)    :15.1812
pow( d, 2 ) :40149.7
```

Random Numbers in C++

There are many cases where you will wish to generate a random number. There are actually two functions you will need to know about random number generation. The first is **rand()**, this function will only return a pseudo random number. The way to fix this is to first call the **srand()** function.

Following is a simple example to generate few random numbers. This example makes use of **time()** function to get the number of seconds on your system time, to randomly seed the rand() function −

```cpp
#include <iostream>
#include <ctime>
#include <cstdlib>

using namespace std;

int main () {
  int i,j;

  // set the seed
  srand( (unsigned)time( NULL ) );

  /* generate 10 random numbers. */
  for( i = 0; i < 10; i++ ) {
    // generate actual random number
    j = rand();
    cout <<" Random Number : " << j << endl;
  }

  return 0;
}
```

When the above code is compiled and executed, it produces the following result −

```
Random Number : 1748144778
Random Number : 630873888
Random Number : 2134540646
Random Number : 219404170
Random Number : 902129458
Random Number : 920445370
Random Number : 1319072661
Random Number : 257938873
Random Number : 1256201101
Random Number : 580322989
```

C++ Arrays

C++ provides a data structure, **the array**, which stores a fixed-size sequential collection of elements of the same type. An array is used to store a collection of data, but it is often more useful to think of an array as a collection of variables of the same type.

Instead of declaring individual variables, such as number0, number1, ..., and number99, you declare one array variable such as numbers and use numbers[0], numbers[1], and ..., numbers[99] to represent individual variables. A specific element in an array is accessed by an index.

All arrays consist of contiguous memory locations. The lowest address corresponds to the first element and the highest address to the last element.

Declaring Arrays

To declare an array in C++, the programmer specifies the type of the elements and the number of elements required by an array as follows −

```
type arrayName [ arraySize ];
```

This is called a single-dimension array. The **arraySize** must be an integer constant greater than zero and **type** can be any valid C++ data type. For example, to declare a 10-element array called balance of type double, use this statement −

```
double balance[10];
```

Initializing Arrays

You can initialize C++ array elements either one by one or using a single statement as follows −

double balance[5] = {1000.0, 2.0, 3.4, 17.0, 50.0};

The number of values between braces { } can not be larger than the number of elements that we declare for the array between square brackets [ ]. Following is an example to assign a single element of the array −

If you omit the size of the array, an array just big enough to hold the initialization is created. Therefore, if you write −

double balance[] = {1000.0, 2.0, 3.4, 17.0, 50.0};

You will create exactly the same array as you did in the previous example.

balance[4] = 50.0;

The above statement assigns element number 5th in the array a value of 50.0. Array with 4th index will be 5th, i.e., last element because all arrays have 0 as the index of their first element which is also called base index. Following is the pictorial representaion of the same array we discussed above −

	0	1	2	3	4
balance	1000.0	2.0	3.4	7.0	50.0

Accessing Array Elements

An element is accessed by indexing the array name. This is done by placing the index of the element within square brackets after the name of the array. For example −

double salary = balance[9];

The above statement will take 10th element from the array and assign the value to salary variable. Following is an example, which will use all the above-mentioned three concepts viz. declaration, assignment and accessing arrays −

```cpp
#include <iostream>
using namespace std;

#include <iomanip>
using std::setw;

int main () {

   int n[ 10 ]; // n is an array of 10 integers

   // initialize elements of array n to 0
   for ( int i = 0; i < 10; i++ ) {
      n[ i ] = i + 100; // set element at location i to i + 100
   }
   cout << "Element" << setw( 13 ) << "Value" << endl;

   // output each array element's value
   for ( int j = 0; j < 10; j++ ) {
      cout << setw( 7 )<< j << setw( 13 ) << n[ j ] << endl;
   }
```

```
return 0;
}
```

This program makes use of **setw()** function to format the output. When the above code is compiled and executed, it produces the following result −

Element	Value
0	100
1	101
2	102
3	103
4	104
5	105
6	106
7	107
8	108
9	109

Arrays in C++

Arrays are important to C++ and should need lots of more detail. There are following few important concepts, which should be clear to a C++ programmer −

Sr.No	Concept & Description
1	Multi-dimensional arrays C++ supports multidimensional arrays. The simplest form of the multidimensional array is the

		two-dimensional array.
2		Pointer to an array You can generate a pointer to the first element of an array by simply specifying the array name, without any index.
3		Passing arrays to functions You can pass to the function a pointer to an array by specifying the array's name without an index.
4		Return array from functions C++ allows a function to return an array.

Multi-dimensional Arrays:

C++ allows multidimensional arrays. Here is the general form of a multidimensional array declaration −

```
type name[size1][size2]...[sizeN];
```

For example, the following declaration creates a three dimensional 5 . 10 . 4 integer array −

```
int threedim[5][10][4];
```

Two-Dimensional Arrays

The simplest form of the multidimensional array is the two-dimensional array. A two-dimensional array is, in essence, a list of one-dimensional arrays. To declare a two-dimensional integer array of size x,y, you would write something as follows −

type arrayName [x][y];

Where **type** can be any valid C++ data type and **arrayName** will be a valid C++ identifier.

A two-dimensional array can be think as a table, which will have x number of rows and y number of columns. A 2-dimensional array **a**, which contains three rows and four columns can be shown as below −

	Column 0	Column 1	Column 2	Column 3
Row 0	a[0][0]	a[0][1]	a[0][2]	a[0][3]
Row 1	a[1][0]	a[1][1]	a[1][2]	a[1][3]
Row 2	a[2][0]	a[2][1]	a[2][2]	a[2][3]

Thus, every element in array a is identified by an element name of the form **a[i][j]**, where a is the name of the array, and i and j are the subscripts that uniquely identify each element in a.

Initializing Two-Dimensional Arrays

Multidimensioned arrays may be initialized by specifying bracketed values for each row.

Following is an array with 3 rows and each row have 4 columns.

```
int a[3][4] = {
  {0, 1, 2, 3} ,   /* initializers for row indexed by 0 */
  {4, 5, 6, 7} ,   /* initializers for row indexed by 1 */
  {8, 9, 10, 11}   /* initializers for row indexed by 2 */
};
```

The nested braces, which indicate the intended row, are optional. The following initialization is equivalent to previous example –

```
int a[3][4] = {0,1,2,3,4,5,6,7,8,9,10,11};
```

Accessing Two-Dimensional Array Elements

An element in 2-dimensional array is accessed by using the subscripts, i.e., row index and column index of the array. For example –

```
int val = a[2][3];
```

The above statement will take 4th element from the 3rd row of the array. You can verify it in the above digram.

```
#include <iostream>
using namespace std;

int main () {
  // an array with 5 rows and 2 columns.
  int a[5][2] = { {0,0}, {1,2}, {2,4}, {3,6},{4,8}};

  // output each array element's value
  for ( int i = 0; i < 5; i++ )
    for ( int j = 0; j < 2; j++ ) {

      cout << "a[" << i << "][" << j << "]: ";
      cout << a[i][j]<< endl;
    }
```

```
    return 0;
}
```

When the above code is compiled and executed, it produces the following result −

```
a[0][0]: 0
a[0][1]: 0
a[1][0]: 1
a[1][1]: 2
a[2][0]: 2
a[2][1]: 4
a[3][0]: 3
a[3][1]: 6
a[4][0]: 4
a[4][1]: 8
```

As explained above, you can have arrays with any number of dimensions, although it is likely that most of the arrays you create will be of one or two dimensions.

Pointer to an Array:

It is most likely that you would not understand this chapter until you go through the chapter related C++ Pointers.

So assuming you have bit understanding on pointers in C++, let us start: An array name is a constant pointer to the first element of the array. Therefore, in the declaration −

```
double balance[50];
```

balance is a pointer to &balance[0], which is the address of the first element of the array balance. Thus, the following program fragment assigns **p** the address of the first element of **balance** −

```
double *p;
double balance[10];

p = balance;
```

It is legal to use array names as constant pointers, and vice versa. Therefore, *(balance + 4) is a legitimate way of accessing the data at balance[4].

Once you store the address of first element in p, you can access array elements using *p, *(p+1), *(p+2) and so on. Below is the example to show all the concepts discussed above −

```
#include <iostream>
using namespace std;

int main () {
   // an array with 5 elements.
   double balance[5] = {1000.0, 2.0, 3.4, 17.0, 50.0};
   double *p;

   p = balance;

   // output each array element's value
   cout << "Array values using pointer " << endl;

   for ( int i = 0; i < 5; i++ ) {
      cout << "*(p + " << i << ") : ";
      cout << *(p + i) << endl;
   }
   cout << "Array values using balance as address " << endl;

   for ( int i = 0; i < 5; i++ ) {
```

```
    cout << "*(balance + " << i << ") : ";
    cout << *(balance + i) << endl;
  }

  return 0;
}
```

When the above code is compiled and executed, it produces the following result –

```
Array values using pointer
*(p + 0) : 1000
*(p + 1) : 2
*(p + 2) : 3.4
*(p + 3) : 17
*(p + 4) : 50
Array values using balance as address
*(balance + 0) : 1000
*(balance + 1) : 2
*(balance + 2) : 3.4
*(balance + 3) : 17
*(balance + 4) : 50
```

In the above example, p is a pointer to double which means it can store address of a variable of double type. Once we have address in p, then ***p** will give us value available at the address stored in p, as we have shown in the above example.

Passing Arrays to Functions:

C++ does not allow to pass an entire array as an argument to a function. However, You can pass a pointer to an array by specifying the array's name without an index.

If you want to pass a single-dimension array as an argument in a function, you would have to declare function formal parameter in one of following three ways and all three declaration methods produce similar results because each tells the compiler that an integer pointer is going to be received.

Formal parameters as a pointer as follows −

```
void myFunction(int *param) {
   .
   .
   .
}
```

Formal parameters as a sized array as follows −

```
void myFunction(int param[10]) {
   .
   .
   .
}
```

Formal parameters as an unsized array as follows −

```
void myFunction(int param[]) {
   .
   .
   .
}
```

Now, consider the following function, which will take an array as an argument along with another argument and based on the passed arguments, it will return average of the numbers passed through the array as follows –

```
double getAverage(int arr[], int size) {
  int i, sum = 0;
  double avg;

  for (i = 0; i < size; ++i) {
    sum += arr[i];
  }
  avg = double(sum) / size;

  return avg;
}
```

Now, let us call the above function as follows –

```
#include <iostream>
using namespace std;

// function declaration:
double getAverage(int arr[], int size);

int main () {
  // an int array with 5 elements.
  int balance[5] = {1000, 2, 3, 17, 50};
  double avg;

  // pass pointer to the array as an argument.
  avg = getAverage( balance, 5 ) ;

  // output the returned value
  cout << "Average value is: " << avg << endl;

  return 0;
}
```

When the above code is compiled together and executed, it produces the following result −

Average value is: 214.4

As you can see, the length of the array doesn't matter as far as the function is concerned because C++ performs no bounds checking for the formal parameters.

Return Array from Functions:

C++ does not allow to return an entire array as an argument to a function. However, you can return a pointer to an array by specifying the array's name without an index.

If you want to return a single-dimension array from a function, you would have to declare a function returning a pointer as in the following example −

```
int * myFunction() {
   .
   .
   .
}
```

Second point to remember is that C++ does not advocate to return the address of a local variable to outside of the function so you would have to define the local variable as **static** variable.

Now, consider the following function, which will generate 10 random numbers and return them using an array and call this function as follows −

```
#include <iostream>
#include <ctime>
```

```cpp
using namespace std;

// function to generate and retrun random numbers.
int * getRandom( ) {

   static int  r[10];

   // set the seed
   srand( (unsigned)time( NULL ) );

   for (int i = 0; i < 10; ++i) {
      r[i] = rand();
      cout << r[i] << endl;
   }

   return r;
}

// main function to call above defined function.
int main () {

   // a pointer to an int.
   int *p;

   p = getRandom();

   for ( int i = 0; i < 10; i++ ) {
      cout << "*(p + " << i << ") : ";
      cout << *(p + i) << endl;
   }

   return 0;
}
```

When the above code is compiled together and executed, it produces result something as follows −

```
624723190
1468735695
807113585
976495677
613357504
1377296355
1530315259
1778906708
1820354158
667126415
*(p + 0) : 624723190
*(p + 1) : 1468735695
*(p + 2) : 807113585
*(p + 3) : 976495677
*(p + 4) : 613357504
*(p + 5) : 1377296355
*(p + 6) : 1530315259
*(p + 7) : 1778906708
*(p + 8) : 1820354158
*(p + 9) : 667126415
```

C++ Strings

C++ provides following two types of string representations −

- The C-style character string.
- The string class type introduced with Standard C++.

The C-Style Character String

The C-style character string originated within the C language and continues to be supported within C++. This string is actually a one-dimensional array of characters which is terminated by a **null** character '\0'. Thus a null-terminated string contains the characters that comprise the string followed by a **null**.

The following declaration and initialization create a string consisting of the word "Hello". To hold the null character at the end of the array, the size of the character array containing the string is one more than the number of characters in the word "Hello."

```
char greeting[6] = {'H', 'e', 'l', 'l', 'o', '\0'};
```

If you follow the rule of array initialization, then you can write the above statement as follows −

```
char greeting[] = "Hello";
```

Following is the memory presentation of above defined string in C/C++ −

Index	0	1	2	3	4	5
Variable	H	e	l	l	o	\0
Address	0x23451	0x23452	0x23453	0x23454	0x23455	0x23456

Actually, you do not place the null character at the end of a string constant. The C++ compiler automatically places the '\0' at the end of the string when it initializes the array. Let us try to print above-mentioned string –

```
#include <iostream>

using namespace std;

int main () {

   char greeting[6] = {'H', 'e', 'l', 'l', 'o', '\0'};

   cout << "Greeting message: ";
   cout << greeting << endl;

   return 0;
}
```

When the above code is compiled and executed, it produces the following result –

Greeting message: Hello

C++ supports a wide range of functions that manipulate null-terminated strings –

Sr.No	Function & Purpose
1	**strcpy(s1, s2);** Copies string s2 into string s1.
2	**strcat(s1, s2);** Concatenates string s2 onto the end of string s1.
3	**strlen(s1);** Returns the length of string s1.
4	**strcmp(s1, s2);** Returns 0 if s1 and s2 are the same; less than 0 if s1<s2; greater than 0 if s1>s2.
5	**strchr(s1, ch);** Returns a pointer to the first occurrence of character ch in string s1.
6	**strstr(s1, s2);** Returns a pointer to the first occurrence of string s2 in string s1.

Following example makes use of few of the above-mentioned functions –

```cpp
#include <iostream>
#include <cstring>

using namespace std;

int main () {

   char str1[10] = "Hello";
   char str2[10] = "World";
   char str3[10];
   int len ;

   // copy str1 into str3
   strcpy( str3, str1);
   cout << "strcpy( str3, str1) : " << str3 << endl;

   // concatenates str1 and str2
   strcat( str1, str2);
   cout << "strcat( str1, str2): " << str1 << endl;

   // total lenghth of str1 after concatenation
   len = strlen(str1);
   cout << "strlen(str1) : " << len << endl;

   return 0;
}
```

When the above code is compiled and executed, it produces result something as follows –

```
strcpy( str3, str1) : Hello
strcat( str1, str2): HelloWorld
strlen(str1) : 10
```

The String Class in C++:

The standard C++ library provides a **string** class type that supports all the operations mentioned above, additionally much more functionality. Let us check the following example –

```cpp
#include <iostream>
#include <string>

using namespace std;

int main () {

   string str1 = "Hello";
   string str2 = "World";
   string str3;
   int  len ;

   // copy str1 into str3
   str3 = str1;
   cout << "str3 : " << str3 << endl;

   // concatenates str1 and str2
   str3 = str1 + str2;
   cout << "str1 + str2 : " << str3 << endl;

   // total length of str3 after concatenation
   len = str3.size();
   cout << "str3.size() : " << len << endl;

   return 0;
}
```

When the above code is compiled and executed, it produces result something as follows −

```
str3 : Hello
str1 + str2 : HelloWorld
str3.size() :  10
```

C++ Pointers

C++ pointers are easy and fun to learn. Some C++ tasks are performed more easily with pointers, and other C++ tasks, such as dynamic memory allocation, cannot be performed without them.

As you know every variable is a memory location and every memory location has its address defined which can be accessed using ampersand (&) operator which denotes an address in memory. Consider the following which will print the address of the variables defined −

```cpp
#include <iostream>

using namespace std;
int main () {
   int var1;
   char var2[10];

   cout << "Address of var1 variable: ";
   cout << &var1 << endl;

   cout << "Address of var2 variable: ";
   cout << &var2 << endl;

   return 0;
}
```

When the above code is compiled and executed, it produces the following result −

```
Address of var1 variable: 0xbfebd5c0
Address of var2 variable: 0xbfebd5b6
```

What are Pointers?

A **pointer** is a variable whose value is the address of another variable. Like any variable or constant, you must declare a pointer before you can work with it. The general form of a pointer variable declaration is −

```
type *var-name;
```

Here, **type** is the pointer's base type; it must be a valid C++ type and **var-name** is the name of the pointer variable. The asterisk you used to declare a pointer is the same asterisk that you use for multiplication. However, in this statement the asterisk is being used to designate a variable as a pointer. Following are the valid pointer declaration −

```
int   *ip;   // pointer to an integer
double *dp;   // pointer to a double
float  *fp;   // pointer to a float
char   *ch    // pointer to character
```

The actual data type of the value of all pointers, whether integer, float, character, or otherwise, is the same, a long hexadecimal number that represents a memory address. The only difference between pointers of different data types is the data type of the variable or constant that the pointer points to.

Using Pointers in C++

There are few important operations, which we will do with the pointers very frequently. **(a)** We define a pointer variable. **(b)** Assign the address of a variable to a pointer. **(c)**Finally access the value at the address available in the pointer variable. This is done by using unary operator * that returns the value of the variable located at the address specified by its operand. Following example makes use of these operations −

```cpp
#include <iostream>

using namespace std;

int main () {
   int  var = 20;   // actual variable declaration.
   int *ip;        // pointer variable

   ip = &var;       // store address of var in pointer variable

   cout << "Value of var variable: ";
   cout << var << endl;

   // print the address stored in ip pointer variable
   cout << "Address stored in ip variable: ";
   cout << ip << endl;

   // access the value at the address available in pointer
   cout << "Value of *ip variable: ";
   cout << *ip << endl;

   return 0;
}
```

When the above code is compiled and executed, it produces result something as follows −

```
Value of var variable: 20
Address stored in ip variable: 0xbfc601ac
Value of *ip variable: 20
```

Pointers in C++

Pointers have many but easy concepts and they are very important to C++ programming. There are following few important pointer concepts which should be clear to a C++ programmer −

Sr.No	Concept & Description
1	Null Pointers C++ supports null pointer, which is a constant with a value of zero defined in several standard libraries.
2	Pointer Arithmetic There are four arithmetic operators that can be used on pointers: ++, --, +, -
3	Pointers vs Arrays There is a close relationship between pointers and arrays.
4	Array of Pointers You can define arrays to hold a number of pointers.

5	Pointer to Pointer
	C++ allows you to have pointer on a pointer and so on.
6	Passing Pointers to Functions
	Passing an argument by reference or by address both enable the passed argument to be changed in the calling function by the called function.
7	Return Pointer from Functions
	C++ allows a function to return a pointer to local variable, static variable and dynamically allocated memory as well.

Null Pointers:

It is always a good practice to assign the pointer NULL to a pointer variable in case you do not have exact address to be assigned. This is done at the time of variable declaration. A pointer that is assigned NULL is called a **null** pointer.

The NULL pointer is a constant with a value of zero defined in several standard libraries, including iostream. Consider the following program −

```
#include <iostream>
```

```
using namespace std;
int main () {
  int *ptr = NULL;
  cout << "The value of ptr is " << ptr ;

  return 0;
}
```

When the above code is compiled and executed, it produces the following result –

The value of ptr is 0

On most of the operating systems, programs are not permitted to access memory at address 0 because that memory is reserved by the operating system. However, the memory address 0 has special significance; it signals that the pointer is not intended to point to an accessible memory location. But by convention, if a pointer contains the null (zero) value, it is assumed to point to nothing.

To check for a null pointer you can use an if statement as follows –

```
if(ptr)    // succeeds if p is not null
if(!ptr)   // succeeds if p is null
```

Thus, if all unused pointers are given the null value and you avoid the use of a null pointer, you can avoid the accidental misuse of an uninitialized pointer. Many times, uninitialized variables hold some junk values and it becomes difficult to debug the program.

Pointer Arithmetic:

As you understood pointer is an address which is a numeric value; therefore, you can perform arithmetic operations on a pointer just as you can a numeric value. There are four arithmetic operators that can be used on pointers: ++, --, +, and -

To understand pointer arithmetic, let us consider that **ptr** is an integer pointer which points to the address 1000. Assuming 32-bit integers, let us perform the following arithmetic operation on the pointer −

```
ptr++
```

the **ptr** will point to the location 1004 because each time ptr is incremented, it will point to the next integer. This operation will move the pointer to next memory location without impacting actual value at the memory location. If ptr points to a character whose address is 1000, then above operation will point to the location 1001 because next character will be available at 1001.

Incrementing a Pointer

We prefer using a pointer in our program instead of an array because the variable pointer can be incremented, unlike the array name which cannot be incremented because it is a constant pointer. The following program increments the variable pointer to access each succeeding element of the array −

```
#include <iostream>

using namespace std;
const int MAX = 3;
```

```
int main () {
  int  var[MAX] = {10, 100, 200};
  int  *ptr;

  // let us have array address in pointer.
  ptr = var;

  for (int i = 0; i < MAX; i++) {
    cout << "Address of var[" << i << "] = ";
    cout << ptr << endl;

    cout << "Value of var[" << i << "] = ";
    cout << *ptr << endl;

    // point to the next location
    ptr++;
  }

  return 0;
}
```

When the above code is compiled and executed, it produces result something as follows –

```
Address of var[0] = 0xbfa088b0
Value of var[0] = 10
Address of var[1] = 0xbfa088b4
Value of var[1] = 100
Address of var[2] = 0xbfa088b8
Value of var[2] = 200
```

Pointers vs Arrays:

Pointers and arrays are strongly related. In fact, pointers and arrays are interchangeable in many cases. For example, a pointer that points to the beginning of an array can access that array by using either pointer arithmetic or array-style indexing. Consider the following program −

```cpp
#include <iostream>

using namespace std;
const int MAX = 3;

int main () {
    int var[MAX] = {10, 100, 200};
    int *ptr;

    // let us have array address in pointer.
    ptr = var;

    for (int i = 0; i < MAX; i++) {
        cout << "Address of var[" << i << "] = ";
        cout << ptr << endl;

        cout << "Value of var[" << i << "] = ";
        cout << *ptr << endl;

        // point to the next location
        ptr++;
    }

    return 0;
}
```

When the above code is compiled and executed, it produces result something as follows −

```
Address of var[0] = 0xbfa088b0
Value of var[0] = 10
Address of var[1] = 0xbfa088b4
Value of var[1] = 100
Address of var[2] = 0xbfa088b8
Value of var[2] = 200
```

However, pointers and arrays are not completely interchangeable.

For example, consider the following program –

```
#include <iostream>

using namespace std;
const int MAX = 3;

int main () {
  int  var[MAX] = {10, 100, 200};

  for (int i = 0; i < MAX; i++) {
    *var = i;   // This is a correct syntax
    var++;      // This is incorrect.
  }

  return 0;
}
```

It is perfectly acceptable to apply the pointer operator * to var but it is illegal to modify var value. The reason for this is that var is a constant that points to the beginning of an array and can not be used as l-value.

Because an array name generates a pointer constant, it can still be used in pointer-style expressions, as long as it is not modified.

For example, the following is a valid statement that assigns var[2] the value 500 −

```
*(var + 2) = 500;
```

Above statement is valid and will compile successfully because var is not changed.

Array of Pointers:

Before we understand the concept of array of pointers, let us consider the following example, which makes use of an array of 3 integers −

```
#include <iostream>

using namespace std;
const int MAX = 3;

int main () {
  int  var[MAX] = {10, 100, 200};

  for (int i = 0; i < MAX; i++) {

    cout << "Value of var[" << i << "] = ";
    cout << var[i] << endl;
  }

  return 0;
}
```

When the above code is compiled and executed, it produces the following result −

```
Value of var[0] = 10
Value of var[1] = 100
Value of var[2] = 200
```

There may be a situation, when we want to maintain an array, which can store pointers to an int or char or any other data type available. Following is the declaration of an array of pointers to an integer −

```
int *ptr[MAX];
```

This declares **ptr** as an array of MAX integer pointers. Thus, each element in ptr, now holds a pointer to an int value. Following example makes use of three integers which will be stored in an array of pointers as follows −

```cpp
#include <iostream>

using namespace std;
const int MAX = 3;

int main () {
  int  var[MAX] = {10, 100, 200};
  int *ptr[MAX];

  for (int i = 0; i < MAX; i++) {
   ptr[i] = &var[i]; // assign the address of integer.
  }

  for (int i = 0; i < MAX; i++) {
    cout << "Value of var[" << i << "] = ";
    cout << *ptr[i] << endl;
  }

  return 0;
}
```

When the above code is compiled and executed, it produces the following result −

```
Value of var[0] = 10
Value of var[1] = 100
Value of var[2] = 200
```

You can also use an array of pointers to character to store a list of strings as follows −

```cpp
#include <iostream>

using namespace std;
const int MAX = 4;

int main () {
const char *names[MAX] = { "Zara Ali", "Hina Ali",
"Nuha Ali", "Sara Ali" };

   for (int i = 0; i < MAX; i++) {
     cout << "Value of names[" << i << "] = ";
     cout << (names + i) << endl;
   }

   return 0;
}
```

When the above code is compiled and executed, it produces the following result −

```
Value of names[0] = 0x7ffd256683c0
Value of names[1] = 0x7ffd256683c8
Value of names[2] = 0x7ffd256683d0
Value of names[3] = 0x7ffd256683d8
```

Pointer to Pointer:

A pointer to a pointer is a form of multiple indirection or a chain of pointers. Normally, a pointer contains the address of a variable. When we define a pointer to a pointer, the first pointer contains the address of the second pointer, which points to the location that contains the actual value as shown below.

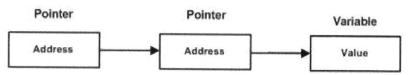

A variable that is a pointer to a pointer must be declared as such. This is done by placing an additional asterisk in front of its name. For example, following is the declaration to declare a pointer to a pointer of type int −

```
int **var;
```

When a target value is indirectly pointed to by a pointer to a pointer, accessing that value requires that the asterisk operator be applied twice, as is shown below in the example −

```
#include <iostream>

using namespace std;

int main () {
    int var;
    int *ptr;
    int **pptr;

    var = 3000;
```

```
// take the address of var
ptr = &var;

// take the address of ptr using address of operator &
pptr = &ptr;

// take the value using pptr
cout << "Value of var :" << var << endl;
cout << "Value available at *ptr :" << *ptr << endl;
cout << "Value available at **pptr :" << **pptr << endl;

return 0;
}
```

When the above code is compiled and executed, it produces the following result –

```
Value of var :3000
Value available at *ptr :3000
Value available at **pptr :3000
```

Passing Pointers to Functions:

C++ allows you to pass a pointer to a function. To do so, simply declare the function parameter as a pointer type.

Following a simple example where we pass an unsigned long pointer to a function and change the value inside the function which reflects back in the calling function –

```
#include <iostream>
#include <ctime>
```

```
using namespace std;
void getSeconds(unsigned long *par);

int main () {
   unsigned long sec;
   getSeconds( &sec );

   // print the actual value
   cout << "Number of seconds :" << sec << endl;

   return 0;
}

void getSeconds(unsigned long *par) {
   // get the current number of seconds
   *par = time( NULL );

   return;
}
```

When the above code is compiled and executed, it produces the following result −

Number of seconds :1294450468

The function which can accept a pointer, can also accept an array as shown in the following example −

```
#include <iostream>
using namespace std;

// function declaration:
double getAverage(int *arr, int size);

int main () {
   // an int array with 5 elements.
   int balance[5] = {1000, 2, 3, 17, 50};
```

```
double avg;

// pass pointer to the array as an argument.
avg = getAverage( balance, 5 ) ;

// output the returned value
cout << "Average value is: " << avg << endl;

return 0;
}

double getAverage(int *arr, int size) {
int i, sum = 0;
double avg;

for (i = 0; i < size; ++i) {
   sum += arr[i];
}
avg = double(sum) / size;

return avg;
}
```

When the above code is compiled together and executed, it produces the following result −

Average value is: 214.4

Return Pointer from Functions:

As we have seen in last chapter how C++ allows to return an array from a function, similar way C++ allows you to return a pointer from a function. To do so, you would have to declare a function returning a pointer as in the following example –

```
int * myFunction() {
  .
  .
  .
}
```

Second point to remember is that, it is not good idea to return the address of a local variable to outside of the function, so you would have to define the local variable as **static** variable.

Now, consider the following function, which will generate 10 random numbers and return them using an array name which represents a pointer i.e., address of first array element.

```
#include <iostream>
#include <ctime>

using namespace std;

// function to generate and retrun random numbers.
int * getRandom( ) {
  static int  r[10];

  // set the seed
  srand( (unsigned)time( NULL ) );

  for (int i = 0; i < 10; ++i) {
```

```
    r[i] = rand();
    cout << r[i] << endl;
  }

  return r;
}

// main function to call above defined function.
int main () {
  // a pointer to an int.
  int *p;

  p = getRandom();
  for ( int i = 0; i < 10; i++ ) {
    cout << "*(p + " << i << ") : ";
    cout << *(p + i) << endl;
  }

  return 0;
}
```

When the above code is compiled together and executed, it produces result something as follows −

```
624723190
1468735695
807113585
976495677
613357504
1377296355
1530315259
1778906708
1820354158
667126415
```

```
*(p + 0) : 624723190
*(p + 1) : 1468735695
*(p + 2) : 807113585
*(p + 3) : 976495677
*(p + 4) : 613357504
*(p + 5) : 1377296355
*(p + 6) : 1530315259
*(p + 7) : 1778906708
*(p + 8) : 1820354158
*(p + 9) : 667126415
```

Decrementing a Pointer:

The same considerations apply to decrementing a pointer, which decreases its value by the number of bytes of its data type as shown below –

```
#include <iostream>

using namespace std;
const int MAX = 3;

int main () {
  int  var[MAX] = {10, 100, 200};
  int *ptr;

  // let us have address of the last element in pointer.
  ptr = &var[MAX-1];

  for (int i = MAX; i > 0; i--) {
    cout << "Address of var[" << i << "] = ";
    cout << ptr << endl;
```

```
cout << "Value of var[" << i << "] = ";
cout << *ptr << endl;

// point to the previous location
ptr--;
}

return 0;
}
```

When the above code is compiled and executed, it produces result something as follows −

```
Address of var[3] = 0xbfdb70f8
Value of var[3] = 200
Address of var[2] = 0xbfdb70f4
Value of var[2] = 100
Address of var[1] = 0xbfdb70f0
Value of var[1] = 10
```

Pointer Comparisons:

Pointers may be compared by using relational operators, such as ==, <, and >. If p1 and p2 point to variables that are related to each other, such as elements of the same array, then p1 and p2 can be meaningfully compared.

The following program modifies the previous example one by incrementing the variable pointer so long as the address to which it points is either less than or equal to the address of the last element of the array, which is &var[MAX - 1] −

```
#include <iostream>

using namespace std;
```

```cpp
const int MAX = 3;

int main () {
  int  var[MAX] = {10, 100, 200};
  int  *ptr;

  // let us have address of the first element in pointer.
  ptr = var;
  int i = 0;

  while ( ptr <= &var[MAX - 1] ) {
    cout << "Address of var[" << i << "] = ";
    cout << ptr << endl;

    cout << "Value of var[" << i << "] = ";
    cout << *ptr << endl;

    // point to the previous location
    ptr++;
    i++;
  }

  return 0;
}
```

When the above code is compiled and executed, it produces result something as follows −

```
Address of var[0] = 0xbfce42d0
Value of var[0] = 10
Address of var[1] = 0xbfce42d4
Value of var[1] = 100
Address of var[2] = 0xbfce42d8
Value of var[2] = 200
```

C++ References

A reference variable is an alias, that is, another name for an already existing variable. Once a reference is initialized with a variable, either the variable name or the reference name may be used to refer to the variable.

References vs Pointers

References are often confused with pointers but three major differences between references and pointers are −

- You cannot have NULL references. You must always be able to assume that a reference is connected to a legitimate piece of storage.

- Once a reference is initialized to an object, it cannot be changed to refer to another object. Pointers can be pointed to another object at any time.

- A reference must be initialized when it is created. Pointers can be initialized at any time.

Creating References in C++

Think of a variable name as a label attached to the variable's location in memory. You can then think of a reference as a second label attached to that memory location. Therefore, you can access the contents of the variable through either the original variable name or the reference.

For example, suppose we have the following example −

```
int i = 17;
```

We can declare reference variables for i as follows.

```
int& r = i;
```

Read the & in these declarations as **reference**. Thus, read the first declaration as "r is an integer reference initialized to i" and read the second declaration as "s is a double reference initialized to d.".

Following example makes use of references on int and double −

```
#include <iostream>

using namespace std;

int main () {
   // declare simple variables
   int   i;
   double d;

   // declare reference variables
   int&   r = i;
   double& s = d;

   i = 5;
   cout << "Value of i : " << i << endl;
   cout << "Value of i reference : " << r  << endl;

   d = 11.7;
   cout << "Value of d : " << d << endl;
   cout << "Value of d reference : " << s  << endl;

   return 0;
}
```

When the above code is compiled together and executed, it produces the following result −

```
Value of i : 5
Value of i reference : 5
Value of d : 11.7
Value of d reference : 11.7
```

References are usually used for function argument lists and function return values. So following are two important subjects related to C++ references which should be clear to a C++ programmer −

Sr.No	Concept & Description
1	References as Parameters C++ supports passing references as function parameter more safely than parameters.
2	Reference as Return Value You can return reference from a C++ function like any other data type.

Parameters by references:

We have discussed how we implement **call by reference** concept using pointers. Here is another example of call by reference which makes use of C++ reference −

```cpp
#include <iostream>
using namespace std;

// function declaration
void swap(int& x, int& y);

int main () {
   // local variable declaration:
   int a = 100;
   int b = 200;

   cout << "Before swap, value of a :" << a << endl;
   cout << "Before swap, value of b :" << b << endl;

   /* calling a function to swap the values.*/
   swap(a, b);

   cout << "After swap, value of a :" << a << endl;
   cout << "After swap, value of b :" << b << endl;

   return 0;
}

// function definition to swap the values.
void swap(int& x, int& y) {

   int temp;
   temp = x; /* save the value at address x */
   x = y;   /* put y into x */
   y = temp; /* put x into y */

   return;
}
```

When the above code is compiled and executed, it produces the following result –

```
Before swap, value of a :100
Before swap, value of b :200
After swap, value of a :200
After swap, value of b :100
```

Returning values by reference:

A C++ program can be made easier to read and maintain by using references rather than pointers. A C++ function can return a reference in a similar way as it returns a pointer.

When a function returns a reference, it returns an implicit pointer to its return value. This way, a function can be used on the left side of an assignment statement. For example, consider this simple program –

```cpp
#include <iostream>
#include <ctime>

using namespace std;

double vals[] = {10.1, 12.6, 33.1, 24.1, 50.0};

double& setValues( int i ) {
   return vals[i];   // return a reference to the ith element
}

// main function to call above defined function.
int main () {
```

```cpp
cout << "Value before change" << endl;
for ( int i = 0; i < 5; i++ ) {
  cout << "vals[" << i << "] = ";
  cout << vals[i] << endl;
}

setValues(1) = 20.23; // change 2nd element
setValues(3) = 70.8;  // change 4th element

cout << "Value after change" << endl;
for ( int i = 0; i < 5; i++ ) {
  cout << "vals[" << i << "] = ";
  cout << vals[i] << endl;
}
return 0;
}
```

When the above code is compiled together and executed, it produces the following result –

```
Value before change
vals[0] = 10.1
vals[1] = 12.6
vals[2] = 33.1
vals[3] = 24.1
vals[4] = 50
Value after change
vals[0] = 10.1
vals[1] = 20.23
vals[2] = 33.1
vals[3] = 70.8
vals[4] = 50
```

When returning a reference, be careful that the object being referred to does not go out of scope. So it is not legal to return a reference to local var. But you can always return a reference on a static variable.

```cpp
int& func() {
  int q;
  //! return q; // Compile time error
  static int x;
  return x;    // Safe, x lives outside this scope
}
```

C++ Date and Time

The C++ standard library does not provide a proper date type. C++ inherits the structs and functions for date and time manipulation from C. To access date and time related functions and structures, you would need to include <ctime> header file in your C++ program.

There are four time-related types: **clock_t, time_t, size_t,** and **tm**. The types - clock_t, size_t and time_t are capable of representing the system time and date as some sort of integer.

The structure type **tm** holds the date and time in the form of a C structure having the following elements –

```
struct tm {
    int tm_sec;   // seconds of minutes from 0 to 61
    int tm_min;   // minutes of hour from 0 to 59
    int tm_hour;  // hours of day from 0 to 24
    int tm_mday;  // day of month from 1 to 31
    int tm_mon;   // month of year from 0 to 11
    int tm_year;  // year since 1900
    int tm_wday;  // days since sunday
    int tm_yday;  // days since January 1st
    int tm_isdst; // hours of daylight savings time
}
```

Following are the important functions, which we use while working with date and time in C or C++. All these functions are part of standard C and C++ library and you can check their detail using reference to C++ standard library given below.

Sr.No	Function & Purpose
1	**time_t time(time_t *time);** This returns the current calendar time of the system in number of seconds elapsed since January 1, 1970. If the system has no time, .1 is returned.
2	**char *ctime(const time_t *time);** This returns a pointer to a string of the form *day month year hours:minutes:seconds year\n\0*.
3	**struct tm *localtime(const time_t *time);** This returns a pointer to the **tm** structure representing local time.
4	**clock_t clock(void);** This returns a value that approximates the amount of time the calling program has been running. A value of .1 is returned if the time is not available.
5	**char * asctime (const struct tm * time);** This returns a pointer to a string that contains the information stored in the structure pointed to by time converted into the form: day month date hours:minutes:seconds year\n\0

6	**struct tm *gmtime(const time_t *time);** This returns a pointer to the time in the form of a tm structure. The time is represented in Coordinated Universal Time (UTC), which is essentially Greenwich Mean Time (GMT).
7	**time_t mktime(struct tm *time);** This returns the calendar-time equivalent of the time found in the structure pointed to by time.
8	**double difftime (time_t time2, time_t time1);** This function calculates the difference in seconds between time1 and time2.
9	**size_t strftime();** This function can be used to format date and time in a specific format.

Current Date and Time

Suppose you want to retrieve the current system date and time, either as a local time or as a Coordinated Universal Time (UTC). Following is the example to achieve the same −

```
#include <iostream>
#include <ctime>

using namespace std;

int main() {
    // current date/time based on current system
    time_t now = time(0);

    // convert now to string form
    char* dt = ctime(&now);

    cout << "The local date and time is: " << dt << endl;

    // convert now to tm struct for UTC
    tm *gmtm = gmtime(&now);
    dt = asctime(gmtm);
    cout << "The UTC date and time is:"<< dt << endl;
}
```

When the above code is compiled and executed, it produces the following result –

The local date and time is: Sat Jan 8 20:07:41 2011

The UTC date and time is:Sun Jan 9 03:07:41 2011

Format Time using struct tm

The **tm** structure is very important while working with date and time in either C or C++. This structure holds the date and time in the form of a C structure as mentioned above. Most of the time related functions makes use of tm structure. Following is an example which makes use of various date and time related functions and tm structure –

While using structure in this chapter, I'm making an assumption that you have basic understanding on C structure and how to access structure members using arrow -> operator.

```cpp
#include <iostream>
#include <ctime>

using namespace std;

int main() {
  // current date/time based on current system
  time_t now = time(0);

  cout << "Number of sec since January 1,1970:" << now << endl;

  tm *ltm = localtime(&now);

  // print various components of tm structure.
  cout << "Year" << 1900 + ltm->tm_year<<endl;
  cout << "Month: "<< 1 + ltm->tm_mon<< endl;
  cout << "Day: "<< ltm->tm_mday << endl;
  cout << "Time: "<< 1 + ltm->tm_hour << ":";
  cout << 1 + ltm->tm_min << ":";
  cout << 1 + ltm->tm_sec << endl;
}
```

When the above code is compiled and executed, it produces the following result −

```
Number of sec since January 1,1970:1563027637
Year2019
Month: 7
Day: 13
Time: 15:21:38
```

C++ Basic Input/Output

The C++ standard libraries provide an extensive set of input/output capabilities which we will see in subsequent chapters. This chapter will discuss very basic and most common I/O operations required for C++ programming.

C++ I/O occurs in streams, which are sequences of bytes. If bytes flow from a device like a keyboard, a disk drive, or a network connection etc. to main memory, this is called **input operation** and if bytes flow from main memory to a device like a display screen, a printer, a disk drive, or a network connection, etc., this is called **output operation**.

I/O Library Header Files

There are following header files important to C++ programs −

Sr.No	Header File & Function and Description
1	**<iostream>** This file defines the **cin, cout, cerr** and **clog** objects, which correspond to the standard input stream, the standard output stream, the un-buffered standard error stream and the buffered standard error stream, respectively.
2	**<iomanip>** This file declares services useful for performing

	formatted I/O with so-called parameterized stream manipulators, such as **setw** and **setprecision**.
3	**<fstream>**
	This file declares services for user-controlled file processing. We will discuss about it in detail in File and Stream related chapter.

The Standard Output Stream (cout)

The predefined object **cout** is an instance of **ostream** class. The cout object is said to be "connected to" the standard output device, which usually is the display screen. The **cout** is used in conjunction with the stream insertion operator, which is written as << which are two less than signs as shown in the following example.

```
#include <iostream>

using namespace std;

int main() {
   char str[] = "Hello C++";

   cout << "Value of str is : " << str << endl;
}
```

When the above code is compiled and executed, it produces the following result −

Value of str is : Hello C++

The C++ compiler also determines the data type of variable to be output and selects the appropriate stream insertion operator to display the value. The << operator is overloaded to output data items of built-in types integer, float, double, strings and pointer values.

The insertion operator << may be used more than once in a single statement as shown above and **endl** is used to add a new-line at the end of the line.

The Standard Input Stream (cin)

The predefined object **cin** is an instance of **istream** class. The cin object is said to be attached to the standard input device, which usually is the keyboard. The **cin** is used in conjunction with the stream extraction operator, which is written as >> which are two greater than signs as shown in the following example.

```
#include <iostream>

using namespace std;

int main() {
   char name[50];

   cout << "Please enter your name: ";
   cin >> name;
   cout << "Your name is: " << name << endl;

}
```

When the above code is compiled and executed, it will prompt you to enter a name. You enter a value and then hit enter to see the following result −

Please enter your name: cplusplus
Your name is: cplusplus

The C++ compiler also determines the data type of the entered value and selects the appropriate stream extraction operator to extract the value and store it in the given variables.

The stream extraction operator >> may be used more than once in a single statement. To request more than one datum you can use the following –

```
cin >> name >> age;
```

This will be equivalent to the following two statements –

```
cin >> name;
cin >> age;
```

The Standard Error Stream (cerr)

The predefined object **cerr** is an instance of **ostream** class. The cerr object is said to be attached to the standard error device, which is also a display screen but the object **cerr** is un-buffered and each stream insertion to cerr causes its output to appear immediately.

The **cerr** is also used in conjunction with the stream insertion operator as shown in the following example.

```
#include <iostream>

using namespace std;

int main() {
```

```
char str[] = "Unable to read....";

cerr << "Error message : " << str << endl;
}
```

When the above code is compiled and executed, it produces the following result –

Error message : Unable to read....

The Standard Log Stream (clog)

The predefined object **clog** is an instance of **ostream** class. The clog object is said to be attached to the standard error device, which is also a display screen but the object **clog** is buffered. This means that each insertion to clog could cause its output to be held in a buffer until the buffer is filled or until the buffer is flushed.

The **clog** is also used in conjunction with the stream insertion operator as shown in the following example.

```
#include <iostream>

using namespace std;

int main() {
  char str[] = "Unable to read....";

  clog << "Error message : " << str << endl;
}
```

When the above code is compiled and executed, it produces the following result −

Error message : Unable to read....

You would not be able to see any difference in cout, cerr and clog with these small examples, but while writing and executing big programs the difference becomes obvious. So it is good practice to display error messages using cerr stream and while displaying other log messages then clog should be used.

C++ Data Structures

C/C++ arrays allow you to define variables that combine several data items of the same kind, but **structure** is another user defined data type which allows you to combine data items of different kinds.

Structures are used to represent a record, suppose you want to keep track of your books in a library. You might want to track the following attributes about each book –

- Title
- Author
- Subject
- Book ID

Defining a Structure

To define a structure, you must use the struct statement. The struct statement defines a new data type, with more than one member, for your program. The format of the struct statement is this –

```
struct [structure tag] {
   member definition;
   member definition;
   ...
   member definition;
} [one or more structure variables];
```

The **structure tag** is optional and each member definition is a normal variable definition, such as int i; or float f; or any other valid variable definition. At the end of the structure's definition, before the final semicolon, you can

specify one or more structure variables but it is optional.
Here is the way you would declare the Book structure –

```
struct Books {
  char  title[50];
  char  author[50];
  char  subject[100];
  int  book_id;
} book;
```

Accessing Structure Members

To access any member of a structure, we use the **member
access operator (.)**. The member access operator is coded
as a period between the structure variable name and the
structure member that we wish to access. You would
use **struct** keyword to define variables of structure type.
Following is the example to explain usage of structure –

```
#include <iostream>
#include <cstring>

using namespace std;

struct Books {
  char  title[50];
  char  author[50];
  char  subject[100];
  int  book_id;
};

int main() {
  struct Books Book1;    // Declare Book1 of type Book
  struct Books Book2;    // Declare Book2 of type Book
```

```
// book 1 specification
strcpy( Book1.title, "Learn C++ Programming");
strcpy( Book1.author, "Chand Miyan");
strcpy( Book1.subject, "C++ Programming");
Book1.book_id = 6495407;

// book 2 specification
strcpy( Book2.title, "Telecom Billing");
strcpy( Book2.author, "Yakit Singha");
strcpy( Book2.subject, "Telecom");
Book2.book_id = 6495700;

// Print Book1 info
cout << "Book 1 title : " << Book1.title <<endl;
cout << "Book 1 author : " << Book1.author <<endl;
cout << "Book 1 subject : " << Book1.subject <<endl;
cout << "Book 1 id : " << Book1.book_id <<endl;

// Print Book2 info
cout << "Book 2 title : " << Book2.title <<endl;
cout << "Book 2 author : " << Book2.author <<endl;
cout << "Book 2 subject : " << Book2.subject <<endl;
cout << "Book 2 id : " << Book2.book_id <<endl;

return 0;
}
```

When the above code is compiled and executed, it produces the following result −

```
Book 1 title : Learn C++ Programming
Book 1 author : Chand Miyan
Book 1 subject : C++ Programming
Book 1 id : 6495407
```

Book 2 title : Telecom Billing
Book 2 author : Yakit Singha
Book 2 subject : Telecom
Book 2 id : 6495700

Structures as Function Arguments

You can pass a structure as a function argument in very similar way as you pass any other variable or pointer. You would access structure variables in the similar way as you have accessed in the above example −

```cpp
#include <iostream>
#include <cstring>

using namespace std;
void printBook( struct Books book );

struct Books {
   char  title[50];
   char  author[50];
   char  subject[100];
   int   book_id;
};

int main() {
   struct Books Book1;      // Declare Book1 of type Book
   struct Books Book2;      // Declare Book2 of type Book

   // book 1 specification
   strcpy( Book1.title, "Learn C++ Programming");
   strcpy( Book1.author, "Chand Miyan");
   strcpy( Book1.subject, "C++ Programming");
   Book1.book_id = 6495407;
```

```cpp
// book 2 specification
strcpy( Book2.title, "Telecom Billing");
strcpy( Book2.author, "Yakit Singha");
strcpy( Book2.subject, "Telecom");
Book2.book_id = 6495700;

// Print Book1 info
printBook( Book1 );

// Print Book2 info
printBook( Book2 );

return 0;
}
void printBook( struct Books book ) {
   cout << "Book title : " << book.title <<endl;
   cout << "Book author : " << book.author <<endl;
   cout << "Book subject : " << book.subject <<endl;
   cout << "Book id : " << book.book_id <<endl;
}
```

When the above code is compiled and executed, it produces the following result –

```
Book title : Learn C++ Programming
Book author : Chand Miyan
Book subject : C++ Programming
Book id : 6495407
Book title : Telecom Billing
Book author : Yakit Singha
Book subject : Telecom
Book id : 6495700
```

Pointers to Structures

You can define pointers to structures in very similar way as you define pointer to any other variable as follows −

```
struct Books *struct_pointer;
```

Now, you can store the address of a structure variable in the above defined pointer variable. To find the address of a structure variable, place the & operator before the structure's name as follows −

```
struct_pointer = &Book1;
```

To access the members of a structure using a pointer to that structure, you must use the -> operator as follows −

```
struct_pointer->title;
```

Let us re-write above example using structure pointer, hope this will be easy for you to understand the concept −

```
#include <iostream>
#include <cstring>

using namespace std;
void printBook( struct Books *book );

struct Books {
   char title[50];
   char author[50];
   char subject[100];
   int book_id;
};
```

```cpp
int main() {
   struct Books Book1;      // Declare Book1 of type Book
   struct Books Book2;      // Declare Book2 of type Book

   // Book 1 specification
   strcpy( Book1.title, "Learn C++ Programming");
   strcpy( Book1.author, "Chand Miyan");
   strcpy( Book1.subject, "C++ Programming");
   Book1.book_id = 6495407;

   // Book 2 specification
   strcpy( Book2.title, "Telecom Billing");
   strcpy( Book2.author, "Yakit Singha");
   strcpy( Book2.subject, "Telecom");
   Book2.book_id = 6495700;

   // Print Book1 info, passing address of structure
   printBook( &Book1 );

   // Print Book1 info, passing address of structure
   printBook( &Book2 );

   return 0;
}

// This function accept pointer to structure as parameter.
void printBook( struct Books *book ) {
   cout << "Book title : " << book->title <<endl;
   cout << "Book author : " << book->author <<endl;
   cout << "Book subject : " << book->subject <<endl;
   cout << "Book id : " << book->book_id <<endl;
}
```

When the above code is compiled and executed, it produces the following result –

```
Book title : Learn C++ Programming
Book author : Chand Miyan
Book subject : C++ Programming
Book id : 6495407
Book title : Telecom Billing
Book author : Yakit Singha
Book subject : Telecom
Book id : 6495700
```

The typedef Keyword

There is an easier way to define structs or you could "alias" types you create.

For example –

```
typedef struct {
   char  title[50];
   char  author[50];
   char  subject[100];
   int   book_id;
} Books;
```

Now, you can use *Books* directly to define variables of *Books* type without using struct keyword.

Following is the example –

```
Books Book1, Book2;
```

You can use **typedef** keyword for non-structs as well as follows –

```
typedef long int *pint32;

pint32 x, y, z;
```

x, y and z are all pointers to long ints.

C++ Classes and Objects

The main purpose of C++ programming is to add object orientation to the C programming language and classes are the central feature of C++ that supports object-oriented programming and are often called user-defined types.

A class is used to specify the form of an object and it combines data representation and methods for manipulating that data into one neat package. The data and functions within a class are called members of the class.

C++ Class Definitions

When you define a class, you define a blueprint for a data type. This doesn't actually define any data, but it does define what the class name means, that is, what an object of the class will consist of and what operations can be performed on such an object.

A class definition starts with the keyword **class** followed by the class name; and the class body, enclosed by a pair of curly braces. A class definition must be followed either by a semicolon or a list of declarations. For example, we defined the Box data type using the keyword **class** as follows −

```
class Box {
  public:
    double length;   // Length of a box
    double breadth;  // Breadth of a box
    double height;   // Height of a box
};
```

The keyword **public** determines the access attributes of the members of the class that follows it. A public member can be accessed from outside the class anywhere within the scope of the class object. You can also specify the members of a class as **private**or **protected** which we will discuss in a sub-section.

Define C++ Objects

A class provides the blueprints for objects, so basically an object is created from a class. We declare objects of a class with exactly the same sort of declaration that we declare variables of basic types. Following statements declare two objects of class Box −

```
Box Box1;       // Declare Box1 of type Box
Box Box2;       // Declare Box2 of type Box
```

Both of the objects Box1 and Box2 will have their own copy of data members.

Accessing the Data Members

The public data members of objects of a class can be accessed using the direct member access operator (.). Let us try the following example to make the things clear −

```
#include <iostream>

using namespace std;

class Box {
  public:
      double length;   // Length of a box
      double breadth;  // Breadth of a box
      double height;   // Height of a box
};
```

```cpp
int main() {
  Box Box1;      // Declare Box1 of type Box
  Box Box2;      // Declare Box2 of type Box
  double volume = 0.0;    // Store the volume of a box here

  // box 1 specification
  Box1.height = 5.0;
  Box1.length = 6.0;
  Box1.breadth = 7.0;

  // box 2 specification
  Box2.height = 10.0;
  Box2.length = 12.0;
  Box2.breadth = 13.0;

  // volume of box 1
  volume = Box1.height * Box1.length * Box1.breadth;
  cout << "Volume of Box1 : " << volume <<endl;

  // volume of box 2
  volume = Box2.height * Box2.length * Box2.breadth;
  cout << "Volume of Box2 : " << volume <<endl;
  return 0;
}
```

When the above code is compiled and executed, it produces the following result −

```
Volume of Box1 : 210
Volume of Box2 : 1560
```

It is important to note that private and protected members can not be accessed directly using direct member access operator (.). We will learn how private and protected members can be accessed.

Classes and Objects in Detail

So far, you have got very basic idea about C++ Classes and Objects. There are further interesting concepts related to C++ Classes and Objects which we will discuss in various sub-sections listed below −

Sr.No	Concept & Description
1	Class Member Functions A member function of a class is a function that has its definition or its prototype within the class definition like any other variable.
2	Class Access Modifiers A class member can be defined as public, private or protected. By default members would be assumed as private.
3	Constructor & Destructor A class constructor is a special function in a class that is called when a new object of the class is created. A destructor is also a special function which is called when created object is deleted.
4	Copy Constructor The copy constructor is a constructor which creates an object by initializing it with an object

	of the same class, which has been created previously.
5	Friend Functions
	A **friend** function is permitted full access to private and protected members of a class.
6	Inline Functions
	With an inline function, the compiler tries to expand the code in the body of the function in place of a call to the function.
7	this Pointer
	Every object has a special pointer **this** which points to the object itself.
8	Pointer to C++ Classes
	A pointer to a class is done exactly the same way a pointer to a structure is. In fact a class is really just a structure with functions in it.
9	Static Members of a Class
	Both data members and function members of a class can be declared as static.

Class Member Functions:

A member function of a class is a function that has its definition or its prototype within the class definition like any other variable. It operates on any object of the class of which it is a member, and has access to all the members of a class for that object.

Let us take previously defined class to access the members of the class using a member function instead of directly accessing them −

```
class Box {
   public:
      double length;      // Length of a box
      double breadth;     // Breadth of a box
      double height;      // Height of a box
      double getVolume(void);// Returns box volume
};
```

Member functions can be defined within the class definition or separately using **scope resolution operator,** : −. Defining a member function within the class definition declares the function **inline**, even if you do not use the inline specifier. So either you can define **Volume()** function as below −

```
class Box {
   public:
      double length;    // Length of a box
      double breadth;   // Breadth of a box
      double height;    // Height of a box

      double getVolume(void) {
        return length * breadth * height;
      }
};
```

If you like, you can define the same function outside the class using the **scope resolution operator** (::) as follows –

```
double Box::getVolume(void) {
  return length * breadth * height;
}
```

Here, only important point is that you would have to use class name just before :: operator. A member function will be called using a dot operator (.) on a object where it will manipulate data related to that object only as follows –

```
Box myBox;        // Create an object
```

```
myBox.getVolume();   // Call member function for the object
```

Let us put above concepts to set and get the value of different class members in a class –

```
#include <iostream>

using namespace std;

class Box {
  public:
      double length;      // Length of a box
      double breadth;     // Breadth of a box
      double height;      // Height of a box

      // Member functions declaration
      double getVolume(void);
      void setLength( double len );
      void setBreadth( double bre );
      void setHeight( double hei );
};
```

```cpp
// Member functions definitions
double Box::getVolume(void) {
  return length * breadth * height;
}

void Box::setLength( double len ) {
  length = len;
}
void Box::setBreadth( double bre ) {
  breadth = bre;
}
void Box::setHeight( double hei ) {
  height = hei;
}

// Main function for the program
int main() {
    Box Box1;          // Declare Box1 of type Box
    Box Box2;          // Declare Box2 of type Box
    double volume = 0.0;    // Store the volume of a box here

    // box 1 specification
    Box1.setLength(6.0);
    Box1.setBreadth(7.0);
    Box1.setHeight(5.0);

    // box 2 specification
    Box2.setLength(12.0);
    Box2.setBreadth(13.0);
    Box2.setHeight(10.0);

    // volume of box 1
    volume = Box1.getVolume();
    cout << "Volume of Box1 : " << volume <<endl;
```

```
// volume of box 2
volume = Box2.getVolume();
cout << "Volume of Box2 : " << volume <<endl;
return 0;
}
```

When the above code is compiled and executed, it produces the following result –

```
Volume of Box1 : 210
Volume of Box2 : 1560
```

Class Access Modifiers:

Data hiding is one of the important features of Object Oriented Programming which allows preventing the functions of a program to access directly the internal representation of a class type. The access restriction to the class members is specified by the labeled **public, private,** and **protected** sections within the class body. The keywords public, private, and protected are called access specifiers.

A class can have multiple public, protected, or private labeled sections. Each section remains in effect until either another section label or the closing right brace of the class body is seen. The default access for members and classes is private.

```
class Base {
  public:
    // public members go here
    protected:

    // protected members go here
    private:
```

```
// private members go here

};
```

The public Members

A **public** member is accessible from anywhere outside the class but within a program. You can set and get the value of public variables without any member function as shown in the following example –

```cpp
#include <iostream>

using namespace std;

class Line {
   public:
      double length;
      void setLength( double len );
      double getLength( void );
};

// Member functions definitions
double Line::getLength(void) {
   return length ;
}

void Line::setLength( double len) {
   length = len;
}

// Main function for the program
int main() {
   Line line;
```

```
// set line length
line.setLength(6.0);
cout << "Length of line : " << line.getLength() <<endl;

// set line length without member function
line.length = 10.0; // OK: because length is public
cout << "Length of line : " << line.length <<endl;

return 0;
}
```

When the above code is compiled and executed, it produces the following result −

```
Length of line : 6
Length of line : 10
```

The private Members

A **private** member variable or function cannot be accessed, or even viewed from outside the class. Only the class and friend functions can access private members.

By default all the members of a class would be private, for example in the following class **width** is a private member, which means until you label a member, it will be assumed a private member −

```
class Box {
  double width;

  public:
    double length;
    void setWidth( double wid );
```

```
    double getWidth( void );
};
```

Practically, we define data in private section and related functions in public section so that they can be called from outside of the class as shown in the following program.

```
#include <iostream>

using namespace std;

class Box {
  public:
    double length;
    void setWidth( double wid );
    double getWidth( void );

  private:
    double width;
};

// Member functions definitions
double Box::getWidth(void) {
  return width ;
}

void Box::setWidth( double wid ) {
  width = wid;
}

// Main function for the program
int main() {
  Box box;
```

```
// set box length without member function
box.length = 10.0; // OK: because length is public
cout << "Length of box : " << box.length <<endl;

// set box width without member function
// box.width = 10.0; // Error: because width is private
box.setWidth(10.0);  // Use member function to set it.
cout << "Width of box : " << box.getWidth() <<endl;

return 0;
}
```

When the above code is compiled and executed, it produces the following result –

```
Length of box : 10
Width of box : 10
```

The protected Members

A **protected** member variable or function is very similar to a private member but it provided one additional benefit that they can be accessed in child classes which are called derived classes.

You will learn derived classes and inheritance in next chapter. For now you can check following example where I have derived one child class **SmallBox** from a parent class **Box**.

Following example is similar to above example and here **width** member will be accessible by any member function of its derived class SmallBox.

```cpp
#include <iostream>
using namespace std;

class Box {
  protected:
    double width;
};

class SmallBox:Box { // SmallBox is the derived class.
  public:
    void setSmallWidth( double wid );
    double getSmallWidth( void );
};

// Member functions of child class
double SmallBox::getSmallWidth(void) {
  return width ;
}

void SmallBox::setSmallWidth( double wid ) {
  width = wid;
}

// Main function for the program
int main() {
  SmallBox box;

  // set box width using member function
  box.setSmallWidth(5.0);
  cout << "Width of box : "<< box.getSmallWidth() <<
endl;

  return 0;
}
```

When the above code is compiled and executed, it produces the following result –

Width of box : 5

Constructor and Destructor:

The Class Constructor

A class **constructor** is a special member function of a class that is executed whenever we create new objects of that class.

A constructor will have exact same name as the class and it does not have any return type at all, not even void. Constructors can be very useful for setting initial values for certain member variables.

Following example explains the concept of constructor –

```cpp
#include <iostream>

using namespace std;

class Line {
  public:
    void setLength( double len );
    double getLength( void );
    Line();  // This is the constructor
  private:
    double length;
};
```

```
// Member functions definitions including constructor
Line::Line(void) {
   cout << "Object is being created" << endl;
}
void Line::setLength( double len ) {
   length = len;
}
double Line::getLength( void ) {
   return length;
}

// Main function for the program
int main() {
   Line line;

   // set line length
   line.setLength(6.0);
   cout << "Length of line : " << line.getLength() <<endl;

   return 0;
}
```

When the above code is compiled and executed, it produces the following result −

```
Object is being created
Length of line : 6
```

Parameterized Constructor

A default constructor does not have any parameter, but if you need, a constructor can have parameters. This helps you to assign initial value to an object at the time of its creation as shown in the following example −

```cpp
#include <iostream>

using namespace std;
class Line {
   public:
      void setLength( double len );
      double getLength( void );
      Line(double len);  // This is the constructor

   private:
      double length;
};

// Member functions definitions including constructor
Line::Line( double len) {
   cout << "Object is being created, length = " << len <<
endl;
   length = len;
}
void Line::setLength( double len ) {
   length = len;
}
double Line::getLength( void ) {
   return length;
}

// Main function for the program
int main() {
   Line line(10.0);

   // get initially set length.
   cout << "Length of line : " << line.getLength() <<endl;
```

```
// set line length again
line.setLength(6.0);
cout << "Length of line : " << line.getLength() <<endl;

return 0;
}
```

When the above code is compiled and executed, it produces the following result −

```
Object is being created, length = 10
Length of line : 10
Length of line : 6
```

Using Initialization Lists to Initialize Fields

In case of parameterized constructor, you can use following syntax to initialize the fields −

```
Line::Line( double len): length(len) {
   cout << "Object is being created, length = " << len <<
endl;
}
```

Above syntax is equal to the following syntax −

```
Line::Line( double len) {
   cout << "Object is being created, length = " << len <<
endl;
   length = len;
}
```

If for a class C, you have multiple fields X, Y, Z, etc., to be initialized, then use can use same syntax and separate the fields by comma as follows −

```
C::C( double a, double b, double c): X(a), Y(b), Z(c) {
   ....
}
```

The Class Destructor

A **destructor** is a special member function of a class that is executed whenever an object of it's class goes out of scope or whenever the delete expression is applied to a pointer to the object of that class.

A destructor will have exact same name as the class prefixed with a tilde (~) and it can neither return a value nor can it take any parameters. Destructor can be very useful for releasing resources before coming out of the program like closing files, releasing memories etc.

Following example explains the concept of destructor −

```cpp
#include <iostream>

using namespace std;
class Line {
  public:
    void setLength( double len );
    double getLength( void );
    Line();  // This is the constructor declaration
    ~Line(); // This is the destructor: declaration

  private:
    double length;
};

// Member functions definitions including constructor
Line::Line(void) {
  cout << "Object is being created" << endl;
```

```
}
Line::~Line(void) {
  cout << "Object is being deleted" << endl;
}
void Line::setLength( double len ) {
  length = len;
}
double Line::getLength( void ) {
  return length;
}

// Main function for the program
int main() {
  Line line;

  // set line length
  line.setLength(6.0);
  cout << "Length of line : " << line.getLength() <<endl;

  return 0;
}
```

When the above code is compiled and executed, it produces the following result −

```
Object is being created
Length of line : 6
Object is being deleted
```

Copy Constructor:

The **copy constructor** is a constructor which creates an object by initializing it with an object of the same class, which has been created previously. The copy constructor is used to −

- Initialize one object from another of the same type.
- Copy an object to pass it as an argument to a function.
- Copy an object to return it from a function.

If a copy constructor is not defined in a class, the compiler itself defines one. If the class has pointer variables and has some dynamic memory allocations, then it is a must to have a copy constructor. The most common form of copy constructor is shown here −

```
classname (const classname &obj) {
   // body of constructor
}
```

Here, **obj** is a reference to an object that is being used to initialize another object.

```
#include <iostream>

using namespace std;

class Line {

   public:
      int getLength( void );
      Line( int len );          // simple constructor
      Line( const Line &obj);  // copy constructor
      ~Line();                  // destructor

   private:
      int *ptr;
};

// Member functions definitions including constructor
```

```cpp
Line::Line(int len) {
  cout << "Normal constructor allocating ptr" << endl;

  // allocate memory for the pointer;
  ptr = new int;
  *ptr = len;
}

Line::Line(const Line &obj) {
  cout << "Copy constructor allocating ptr." << endl;
  ptr = new int;
  *ptr = *obj.ptr; // copy the value
}

Line::~Line(void) {
  cout << "Freeing memory!" << endl;
  delete ptr;
}

int Line::getLength( void ) {
  return *ptr;
}

void display(Line obj) {
  cout << "Length of line : " << obj.getLength() <<endl;
}

// Main function for the program
int main() {
  Line line(10);

  display(line);

  return 0;
}
```

When the above code is compiled and executed, it produces the following result –

```
Normal constructor allocating ptr
Copy constructor allocating ptr.
Length of line : 10
Freeing memory!
Freeing memory!
```

Let us see the same example but with a small change to create another object using existing object of the same type –

```cpp
#include <iostream>

using namespace std;

class Line {
   public:
      int getLength( void );
      Line( int len );            // simple constructor
      Line( const Line &obj);  // copy constructor
      ~Line();                    // destructor

   private:
      int *ptr;
};

// Member functions definitions including constructor
Line::Line(int len) {
   cout << "Normal constructor allocating ptr" << endl;

   // allocate memory for the pointer;
   ptr = new int;
   *ptr = len;
```

```
}

Line::Line(const Line &obj) {
  cout << "Copy constructor allocating ptr." << endl;
  ptr = new int;
  *ptr = *obj.ptr; // copy the value
}

Line::~Line(void) {
  cout << "Freeing memory!" << endl;
  delete ptr;
}

int Line::getLength( void ) {
  return *ptr;
}

void display(Line obj) {
  cout << "Length of line : " << obj.getLength() <<endl;
}

// Main function for the program
int main() {

  Line line1(10);

  Line line2 = line1; // This also calls copy constructor

  display(line1);
  display(line2);

  return 0;
}
```

When the above code is compiled and executed, it produces the following result −

```
Normal constructor allocating ptr
Copy constructor allocating ptr.
Copy constructor allocating ptr.
Length of line : 10
Freeing memory!
Copy constructor allocating ptr.
Length of line : 10
Freeing memory!
Freeing memory!
Freeing memory!
```

Friend Functions:

A friend function of a class is defined outside that class' scope but it has the right to access all private and protected members of the class. Even though the prototypes for friend functions appear in the class definition, friends are not member functions.

A friend can be a function, function template, or member function, or a class or class template, in which case the entire class and all of its members are friends.

To declare a function as a friend of a class, precede the function prototype in the class definition with keyword **friend** as follows −

```cpp
class Box {
  double width;

  public:
    double length;
    friend void printWidth( Box box );
```

```
   void setWidth( double wid );
};
```

To declare all member functions of class ClassTwo as friends of class ClassOne, place a following declaration in the definition of class ClassOne −

```
friend class ClassTwo;
```

Consider the following program −

```cpp
#include <iostream>

using namespace std;

class Box {
  double width;

  public:
    friend void printWidth( Box box );
    void setWidth( double wid );
};

// Member function definition
void Box::setWidth( double wid ) {
  width = wid;
}

// Note: printWidth() is not a member function of any class.
void printWidth( Box box ) {
  /* Because printWidth() is a friend of Box, it can
  directly access any member of this class */
  cout << "Width of box : " << box.width <<endl;
}
```

```
// Main function for the program
int main() {
   Box box;

   // set box width without member function
   box.setWidth(10.0);

   // Use friend function to print the wdith.
   printWidth( box );

   return 0;
}
```

When the above code is compiled and executed, it produces the following result –

Width of box : 10

C++ Inheritance

One of the most important concepts in object-oriented programming is that of inheritance. Inheritance allows us to define a class in terms of another class, which makes it easier to create and maintain an application. This also provides an opportunity to reuse the code functionality and fast implementation time.

When creating a class, instead of writing completely new data members and member functions, the programmer can designate that the new class should inherit the members of an existing class. This existing class is called the **base** class, and the new class is referred to as the **derived** class.

The idea of inheritance implements the **is a** relationship. For example, mammal IS-A animal, dog IS-A mammal hence dog IS-A animal as well and so on.

Base and Derived Classes

A class can be derived from more than one classes, which means it can inherit data and functions from multiple base classes. To define a derived class, we use a class derivation list to specify the base class(es). A class derivation list names one or more base classes and has the form −

class derived-class: access-specifier base-class

Where access-specifier is one of **public, protected,** or **private**, and base-class is the name of a previously defined class. If the access-specifier is not used, then it is private by default.

Consider a base class **Shape** and its derived class **Rectangle** as follows −

```cpp
#include <iostream>

using namespace std;

// Base class
class Shape {
  public:
    void setWidth(int w) {
      width = w;
    }
    void setHeight(int h) {
      height = h;
    }

  protected:
    int width;
    int height;
};

// Derived class
class Rectangle: public Shape {
  public:
    int getArea() {
      return (width * height);
    }
};

int main(void) {
  Rectangle Rect;

  Rect.setWidth(5);
  Rect.setHeight(7);
```

```
// Print the area of the object.
cout << "Total area: " << Rect.getArea() << endl;

return 0;
}
```

When the above code is compiled and executed, it produces the following result −

Total area: 35

Access Control and Inheritance

A derived class can access all the non-private members of its base class. Thus base-class members that should not be accessible to the member functions of derived classes should be declared private in the base class.

We can summarize the different access types according to - who can access them in the following way −

Access	public	protected	private
Same class	yes	yes	yes
Derived classes	yes	yes	no
Outside	yes	no	no

classes

A derived class inherits all base class methods with the following exceptions −

- Constructors, destructors and copy constructors of the base class.
- Overloaded operators of the base class.
- The friend functions of the base class.

Type of Inheritance

When deriving a class from a base class, the base class may be inherited through **public, protected** or **private** inheritance. The type of inheritance is specified by the access-specifier as explained above.

We hardly use **protected** or **private** inheritance, but **public** inheritance is commonly used. While using different type of inheritance, following rules are applied −

- **Public Inheritance** − When deriving a class from a **public** base class, **public** members of the base class become **public** members of the derived class and **protected** members of the base class become **protected** members of the derived class. A base class's **private** members are never accessible directly from a derived class, but can be accessed through calls to the **public** and **protected** members of the base class.

- **Protected Inheritance** – When deriving from a **protected** base
class, **public**and **protected** members of the base class become **protected** members of the derived class.

- **Private Inheritance** – When deriving from a **private** base
class, **public** and **protected** members of the base class become **private** members of the derived class.

Multiple Inheritance

A C++ class can inherit members from more than one class and here is the extended syntax –

class derived-class: access baseA, access baseB....

Where access is one of **public, protected,** or **private** and would be given for every base class and they will be separated by comma as shown above. Let us try the following example –

```cpp
#include <iostream>

using namespace std;

// Base class Shape
class Shape {
  public:
    void setWidth(int w) {
      width = w;
    }
    void setHeight(int h) {
      height = h;
```

```cpp
    }

  protected:
    int width;
    int height;
};

// Base class PaintCost
class PaintCost {
  public:
    int getCost(int area) {
      return area * 70;
    }
};

// Derived class
class Rectangle: public Shape, public PaintCost {
  public:
    int getArea() {
      return (width * height);
    }
};

int main(void) {
  Rectangle Rect;
  int area;

  Rect.setWidth(5);
  Rect.setHeight(7);

  area = Rect.getArea();

  // Print the area of the object.
  cout << "Total area: " << Rect.getArea() << endl;
```

```
// Print the total cost of painting
cout << "Total paint cost: $" << Rect.getCost(area) <<
endl;

   return 0;
}
```

When the above code is compiled and executed, it produces the following result −

```
Total area: 35
Total paint cost: $2450
```

C++ Overloading (Operator and Function)

C++ allows you to specify more than one definition for a **function** name or an **operator**in the same scope, which is called **function overloading** and **operator overloading** respectively.

An overloaded declaration is a declaration that is declared with the same name as a previously declared declaration in the same scope, except that both declarations have different arguments and obviously different definition (implementation).

When you call an overloaded **function** or **operator**, the compiler determines the most appropriate definition to use, by comparing the argument types you have used to call the function or operator with the parameter types specified in the definitions. The process of selecting the most appropriate overloaded function or operator is called **overload resolution**.

Function Overloading in C++

You can have multiple definitions for the same function name in the same scope. The definition of the function must differ from each other by the types and/or the number of arguments in the argument list. You cannot overload function declarations that differ only by return type.

Following is the example where same function **print()** is being used to print different data types −

```cpp
#include <iostream>
using namespace std;

class printData {
  public:
    void print(int i) {
      cout << "Printing int: " << i << endl;
    }
    void print(double  f) {
      cout << "Printing float: " << f << endl;
    }
    void print(char* c) {
      cout << "Printing character: " << c << endl;
    }
};

int main(void) {
  printData pd;

  // Call print to print integer
  pd.print(5);

  // Call print to print float
  pd.print(500.263);

  // Call print to print character
  pd.print("Hello C++");

  return 0;
}
```

When the above code is compiled and executed, it produces the following result −

```
Printing int: 5
Printing float: 500.263
Printing character: Hello C++
```

Operators Overloading in C++

You can redefine or overload most of the built-in operators available in C++. Thus, a programmer can use operators with user-defined types as well.

Overloaded operators are functions with special names: the keyword "operator" followed by the symbol for the operator being defined. Like any other function, an overloaded operator has a return type and a parameter list.

```
Box operator+(const Box&);
```

declares the addition operator that can be used to **add** two Box objects and returns final Box object. Most overloaded operators may be defined as ordinary non-member functions or as class member functions. In case we define above function as non-member function of a class then we would have to pass two arguments for each operand as follows −

```
Box operator+(const Box&, const Box&);
```

Following is the example to show the concept of operator over loading using a member function. Here an object is passed as an argument whose properties will be accessed using this object, the object which will call this operator can be accessed using **this**operator as explained below −

```cpp
#include <iostream>
using namespace std;

class Box {
  public:
    double getVolume(void) {
      return length * breadth * height;
    }
    void setLength( double len ) {
      length = len;
    }
    void setBreadth( double bre ) {
      breadth = bre;
    }
    void setHeight( double hei ) {
      height = hei;
    }

    // Overload + operator to add two Box objects.
    Box operator+(const Box& b) {
      Box box;
      box.length = this->length + b.length;
      box.breadth = this->breadth + b.breadth;
      box.height = this->height + b.height;
      return box;
    }

  private:
    double length;      // Length of a box
    double breadth;     // Breadth of a box
    double height;      // Height of a box
};

// Main function for the program
int main() {
```

```cpp
Box Box1;              // Declare Box1 of type Box
Box Box2;              // Declare Box2 of type Box
Box Box3;              // Declare Box3 of type Box
double volume = 0.0;   // Store the volume of a box here

// box 1 specification
Box1.setLength(6.0);
Box1.setBreadth(7.0);
Box1.setHeight(5.0);

// box 2 specification
Box2.setLength(12.0);
Box2.setBreadth(13.0);
Box2.setHeight(10.0);

// volume of box 1
volume = Box1.getVolume();
cout << "Volume of Box1 : " << volume <<endl;

// volume of box 2
volume = Box2.getVolume();
cout << "Volume of Box2 : " << volume <<endl;

// Add two object as follows:
Box3 = Box1 + Box2;

// volume of box 3
volume = Box3.getVolume();
cout << "Volume of Box3 : " << volume <<endl;

return 0;
}
```

When the above code is compiled and executed, it produces the following result –

```
Volume of Box1 : 210
Volume of Box2 : 1560
Volume of Box3 : 5400
```

Overloadable/Non-overloadableOperators

Following is the list of operators which can be overloaded

—

+	-	*	/	%	^
&	|	~	!	,	=
<	>	<=	>=	++	--
<<	>>	==	!=	&&	||
+=	-=	/=	%=	^=	&=
|=	*=	<<=	>>=	[]	()
->	->*	new	new []	delete	delete []

Following is the list of operators, which can not be overloaded −

::	.*	.	?:

Polymorphism in C++

The word **polymorphism** means having many forms. Typically, polymorphism occurs when there is a hierarchy of classes and they are related by inheritance.

C++ polymorphism means that a call to a member function will cause a different function to be executed depending on the type of object that invokes the function.

Consider the following example where a base class has been derived by other two classes −

```cpp
#include <iostream>
using namespace std;

class Shape {
   protected:
      int width, height;

   public:
      Shape( int a = 0, int b = 0){
         width = a;
         height = b;
      }
      int area() {
         cout << "Parent class area :" <<endl;
         return 0;
      }
};
class Rectangle: public Shape {
   public:
      Rectangle( int a = 0, int b = 0):Shape(a, b) { }
```

```cpp
      int area () {
        cout << "Rectangle class area :" <<endl;
        return (width * height);
      }
};

class Triangle: public Shape {
  public:
    Triangle( int a = 0, int b = 0):Shape(a, b) { }

    int area () {
      cout << "Triangle class area :" <<endl;
      return (width * height / 2);
    }
};

// Main function for the program
int main() {
  Shape *shape;
  Rectangle rec(10,7);
  Triangle  tri(10,5);

  // store the address of Rectangle
  shape = &rec;

  // call rectangle area.
  shape->area();

  // store the address of Triangle
  shape = &tri;

  // call triangle area.
  shape->area();
```

```
return 0;
}
```

When the above code is compiled and executed, it produces the following result −

Parent class area :
Parent class area :

The reason for the incorrect output is that the call of the function area() is being set once by the compiler as the version defined in the base class. This is called **static resolution** of the function call, or **static linkage** - the function call is fixed before the program is executed. This is also sometimes called **early binding** because the area() function is set during the compilation of the program.

But now, let's make a slight modification in our program and precede the declaration of area() in the Shape class with the keyword **virtual** so that it looks like this −

```
class Shape {
  protected:
    int width, height;

  public:
    Shape( int a = 0, int b = 0) {
      width = a;
      height = b;
    }
    virtual int area() {
      cout << "Parent class area :" <<endl;
      return 0;
    }
};
```

After this slight modification, when the previous example code is compiled and executed, it produces the following result –

Rectangle class area
Triangle class area

This time, the compiler looks at the contents of the pointer instead of it's type. Hence, since addresses of objects of tri and rec classes are stored in *shape the respective area() function is called.

As you can see, each of the child classes has a separate implementation for the function area(). This is how **polymorphism** is generally used. You have different classes with a function of the same name, and even the same parameters, but with different implementations.

Virtual Function

A **virtual** function is a function in a base class that is declared using the keyword **virtual**. Defining in a base class a virtual function, with another version in a derived class, signals to the compiler that we don't want static linkage for this function.

What we do want is the selection of the function to be called at any given point in the program to be based on the kind of object for which it is called. This sort of operation is referred to as **dynamic linkage**, or **late binding**.

Pure Virtual Functions

It is possible that you want to include a virtual function in a base class so that it may be redefined in a derived class to suit the objects of that class, but that there is no meaningful definition you could give for the function in the base class.

We can change the virtual function area() in the base class to the following −

```cpp
class Shape {
  protected:
    int width, height;

  public:
    Shape(int a = 0, int b = 0) {
      width = a;
      height = b;
    }

    // pure virtual function
    virtual int area() = 0;
};
```

The = 0 tells the compiler that the function has no body and above virtual function will be called **pure virtual function**.

Data Abstraction in C++

Data abstraction refers to providing only essential information to the outside world and hiding their background details, i.e., to represent the needed information in program without presenting the details.

Data abstraction is a programming (and design) technique that relies on the separation of interface and implementation.

Let's take one real life example of a TV, which you can turn on and off, change the channel, adjust the volume, and add external components such as speakers, VCRs, and DVD players, BUT you do not know its internal details, that is, you do not know how it receives signals over the air or through a cable, how it translates them, and finally displays them on the screen.

Thus, we can say a television clearly separates its internal implementation from its external interface and you can play with its interfaces like the power button, channel changer, and volume control without having any knowledge of its internals.

In C++, classes provides great level of **data abstraction**. They provide sufficient public methods to the outside world to play with the functionality of the object and to manipulate object data, i.e., state without actually knowing how class has been implemented internally.

For example, your program can make a call to the **sort()** function without knowing what algorithm the function actually uses to sort the given values. In fact, the underlying implementation of the sorting functionality could change between releases of the library, and as long as the interface stays the same, your function call will still work.

In C++, we use **classes** to define our own abstract data types (ADT). You can use the **cout** object of class **ostream** to stream data to standard output like this −

```
#include <iostream>
using namespace std;

int main() {
    cout << "Hello C++" <<endl;
    return 0;
}
```

Here, you don't need to understand how **cout** displays the text on the user's screen. You need to only know the public interface and the underlying implementation of 'cout' is free to change.

Access Labels Enforce Abstraction

In C++, we use access labels to define the abstract interface to the class. A class may contain zero or more access labels −

- Members defined with a public label are accessible to all parts of the program. The data-abstraction view of a type is defined by its public members.

- Members defined with a private label are not accessible to code that uses the class. The private sections hide the implementation from code that uses the type.

There are no restrictions on how often an access label may appear. Each access label specifies the access level of the succeeding member definitions. The specified access level remains in effect until the next access label is encountered or the closing right brace of the class body is seen.

Benefits of Data Abstraction

Data abstraction provides two important advantages −

- Class internals are protected from inadvertent user-level errors, which might corrupt the state of the object.

- The class implementation may evolve over time in response to changing requirements or bug reports without requiring change in user-level code.

By defining data members only in the private section of the class, the class author is free to make changes in the data. If the implementation changes, only the class code needs to be examined to see what affect the change may have. If data is public, then any function that directly access the data members of the old representation might be broken.

Data Abstraction Example

Any C++ program where you implement a class with public and private members is an example of data abstraction. Consider the following example −

```
#include <iostream>
using namespace std;

class Adder {
  public:
    // constructor
```

```cpp
      Adder(int i = 0) {
        total = i;
      }

      // interface to outside world
      void addNum(int number) {
        total += number;
      }

      // interface to outside world
      int getTotal() {
        return total;
      };

   private:
      // hidden data from outside world
      int total;
};

int main() {
   Adder a;

   a.addNum(10);
   a.addNum(20);
   a.addNum(30);

   cout << "Total " << a.getTotal() <<endl;
   return 0;
}
```

When the above code is compiled and executed, it produces the following result –

Total 60

Above class adds numbers together, and returns the sum. The public members - **addNum** and **getTotal** are the interfaces to the outside world and a user needs to know them to use the class. The private member **total** is something that the user doesn't need to know about, but is needed for the class to operate properly.

Designing Strategy

Abstraction separates code into interface and implementation. So while designing your component, you must keep interface independent of the implementation so that if you change underlying implementation then interface would remain intact.

In this case whatever programs are using these interfaces, they would not be impacted and would just need a recompilation with the latest implementation.

Data Encapsulation in C++

All C++ programs are composed of the following two fundamental elements –

- **Program statements (code)** – This is the part of a program that performs actions and they are called functions.

- **Program data** – The data is the information of the program which gets affected by the program functions.

Encapsulation is an Object Oriented Programming concept that binds together the data and functions that manipulate the data, and that keeps both safe from outside interference and misuse. Data encapsulation led to the important OOP concept of **data hiding**.

Data encapsulation is a mechanism of bundling the data, and the functions that use them and **data abstraction** is a mechanism of exposing only the interfaces and hiding the implementation details from the user.

C++ supports the properties of encapsulation and data hiding through the creation of user-defined types, called **classes**. We already have studied that a class can contain **private,** **protected** and **public** members. By default, all items defined in a class are private.

For example –

```
class Box {
  public:
    double getVolume(void) {
      return length * breadth * height;
    }
```

```
private:
    double length;    // Length of a box
    double breadth;   // Breadth of a box
    double height;    // Height of a box
};
```

The variables length, breadth, and height are **private**. This means that they can be accessed only by other members of the Box class, and not by any other part of your program. This is one way encapsulation is achieved.

To make parts of a class **public** (i.e., accessible to other parts of your program), you must declare them after the **public** keyword. All variables or functions defined after the public specifier are accessible by all other functions in your program.

Making one class a friend of another exposes the implementation details and reduces encapsulation. The ideal is to keep as many of the details of each class hidden from all other classes as possible.

Data Encapsulation Example

Any C++ program where you implement a class with public and private members is an example of data encapsulation and data abstraction.

Consider the following example –

```
#include <iostream>
using namespace std;

class Adder {
  public:
    // constructor
    Adder(int i = 0) {
```

```cpp
      total = i;
    }

    // interface to outside world
    void addNum(int number) {
      total += number;
    }

    // interface to outside world
    int getTotal() {
      return total;
    };

  private:
    // hidden data from outside world
    int total;
};

int main() {
  Adder a;

  a.addNum(10);
  a.addNum(20);
  a.addNum(30);

  cout << "Total " << a.getTotal() <<endl;
  return 0;
}
```

When the above code is compiled and executed, it produces the following result −

Total 60

Above class adds numbers together, and returns the sum. The public members **addNum** and **getTotal** are the interfaces to the outside world and a user needs to know them to use the class. The private member **total** is something that is hidden from the outside world, but is needed for the class to operate properly.

Designing Strategy

Most of us have learnt to make class members private by default unless we really need to expose them. That's just good **encapsulation**.

This is applied most frequently to data members, but it applies equally to all members, including virtual functions.

Interfaces in C++ (Abstract Classes)

An interface describes the behavior or capabilities of a C++ class without committing to a particular implementation of that class.

The C++ interfaces are implemented using **abstract classes** and these abstract classes should not be confused with data abstraction which is a concept of keeping implementation details separate from associated data.

A class is made abstract by declaring at least one of its functions as **pure virtual**function. A pure virtual function is specified by placing "= 0" in its declaration as follows –

```cpp
class Box {
   public:
      // pure virtual function
      virtual double getVolume() = 0;

   private:
      double length;      // Length of a box
      double breadth;     // Breadth of a box
      double height;      // Height of a box
};
```

The purpose of an **abstract class** (often referred to as an ABC) is to provide an appropriate base class from which other classes can inherit. Abstract classes cannot be used to instantiate objects and serves only as an **interface**. Attempting to instantiate an object of an abstract class causes a compilation error.

Thus, if a subclass of an ABC needs to be instantiated, it has to implement each of the virtual functions, which means that it supports the interface declared by the ABC. Failure to override a pure virtual function in a derived class, then attempting to instantiate objects of that class, is a compilation error.

Classes that can be used to instantiate objects are called **concrete classes**.

Abstract Class Example

Consider the following example where parent class provides an interface to the base class to implement a function called **getArea()** −

```cpp
#include <iostream>

using namespace std;

// Base class
class Shape {
  public:
    // pure virtual function providing interface framework.
    virtual int getArea() = 0;
    void setWidth(int w) {
      width = w;
    }

    void setHeight(int h) {
      height = h;
    }

  protected:
    int width;
    int height;
};

// Derived classes
```

```cpp
class Rectangle: public Shape {
  public:
    int getArea() {
      return (width * height);
    }
};

class Triangle: public Shape {
  public:
    int getArea() {
      return (width * height)/2;
    }
};

int main(void) {
  Rectangle Rect;
  Triangle  Tri;

  Rect.setWidth(5);
  Rect.setHeight(7);

  // Print the area of the object.
  cout << "Total Rectangle area: " << Rect.getArea() << endl;

  Tri.setWidth(5);
  Tri.setHeight(7);

  // Print the area of the object.
  cout << "Total Triangle area: " << Tri.getArea() << endl;

  return 0;
}
```

When the above code is compiled and executed, it produces the following result −

```
Total Rectangle area: 35
Total Triangle area: 17
```

You can see how an abstract class defined an interface in terms of getArea() and two other classes implemented same function but with different algorithm to calculate the area specific to the shape.

Designing Strategy

An object-oriented system might use an abstract base class to provide a common and standardized interface appropriate for all the external applications. Then, through inheritance from that abstract base class, derived classes are formed that operate similarly.

The capabilities (i.e., the public functions) offered by the external applications are provided as pure virtual functions in the abstract base class. The implementations of these pure virtual functions are provided in the derived classes that correspond to the specific types of the application.

This architecture also allows new applications to be added to a system easily, even after the system has been defined.

C++ Files and Streams

So far, we have been using the **iostream** standard library, which provides **cin** and **cout**methods for reading from standard input and writing to standard output respectively.

This tutorial will teach you how to read and write from a file. This requires another standard C++ library called **fstream**, which defines three new data types −

Sr.No	Data Type & Description
1	**ofstream** This data type represents the output file stream and is used to create files and to write information to files.
2	**ifstream** This data type represents the input file stream and is used to read information from files.
3	**fstream** This data type represents the file stream generally, and has the capabilities of both ofstream and ifstream which means it can create files, write information to files, and read information from files.

To perform file processing in C++, header files <iostream> and <fstream> must be included in your C++ source file.

Opening a File

A file must be opened before you can read from it or write to it. Either **ofstream** or **fstream** object may be used to open a file for writing. And ifstream object is used to open a file for reading purpose only.

Following is the standard syntax for open() function, which is a member of fstream, ifstream, and ofstream objects.

void open(const char *filename, ios::openmode mode);

Here, the first argument specifies the name and location of the file to be opened and the second argument of the **open()** member function defines the mode in which the file should be opened.

Sr.No	Mode Flag & Description
1	**ios::app** Append mode. All output to that file to be appended to the end.
2	**ios::ate** Open a file for output and move the read/write control to the end of the file.

3	ios::in Open a file for reading.
4	ios::out Open a file for writing.
5	ios::trunc If the file already exists, its contents will be truncated before opening the file.

You can combine two or more of these values by **OR**ing them together. For example if you want to open a file in write mode and want to truncate it in case that already exists, following will be the syntax –

```
ofstream outfile;
outfile.open("file.dat", ios::out | ios::trunc );
```

Similar way, you can open a file for reading and writing purpose as follows –

```
fstream afile;
afile.open("file.dat", ios::out | ios::in );
```

Closing a File

When a C++ program terminates it automatically flushes all the streams, release all the allocated memory and close all the opened files. But it is always a good practice that a programmer should close all the opened files before program termination.

Following is the standard syntax for close() function, which is a member of fstream, ifstream, and ofstream objects.

void close();

Writing to a File

While doing C++ programming, you write information to a file from your program using the stream insertion operator (<<) just as you use that operator to output information to the screen. The only difference is that you use an **ofstream** or **fstream** object instead of the **cout** object.

Reading from a File

You read information from a file into your program using the stream extraction operator (>>) just as you use that operator to input information from the keyboard. The only difference is that you use an **ifstream** or **fstream** object instead of the **cin** object.

Read and Write Example

Following is the C++ program which opens a file in reading and writing mode. After writing information entered by the user to a file named afile.dat, the program reads information from the file and outputs it onto the screen −

```
#include <fstream>
#include <iostream>
using namespace std;
```

```cpp
int main () {
  char data[100];

  // open a file in write mode.
  ofstream outfile;
  outfile.open("afile.dat");

  cout << "Writing to the file" << endl;
  cout << "Enter your name: ";
  cin.getline(data, 100);

  // write inputted data into the file.
  outfile << data << endl;

  cout << "Enter your age: ";
  cin >> data;
  cin.ignore();

  // again write inputted data into the file.
  outfile << data << endl;

  // close the opened file.
  outfile.close();

  // open a file in read mode.
  ifstream infile;
  infile.open("afile.dat");

  cout << "Reading from the file" << endl;
  infile >> data;

  // write the data at the screen.
  cout << data << endl;

  // again read the data from the file and display it.
```

```
infile >> data;
cout << data << endl;

// close the opened file.
infile.close();

return 0;
}
```

When the above code is compiled and executed, it produces the following sample input and output −

```
$./a.out
Writing to the file
Enter your name: Zara
Enter your age: 9
Reading from the file
Zara
9
```

Above examples make use of additional functions from cin object, like getline() function to read the line from outside and ignore() function to ignore the extra characters left by previous read statement.

File Position Pointers

Both **istream** and **ostream** provide member functions for repositioning the file-position pointer. These member functions are **seekg** ("seek get") for istream and **seekp** ("seek put") for ostream.

The argument to seekg and seekp normally is a long integer. A second argument can be specified to indicate the seek direction. The seek direction can be **ios::beg** (the default) for positioning relative to the beginning of a stream, **ios::cur** for positioning relative to the current position in a stream or **ios::end** for positioning relative to the end of a stream.

The file-position pointer is an integer value that specifies the location in the file as a number of bytes from the file's starting location. Some examples of positioning the "get" file-position pointer are −

```
// position to the nth byte of fileObject (assumes ios::beg)
fileObject.seekg( n );

// position n bytes forward in fileObject
fileObject.seekg( n, ios::cur );

// position n bytes back from end of fileObject
fileObject.seekg( n, ios::end );

// position at end of fileObject
fileObject.seekg( 0, ios::end );
```

C++ Exception Handling

An exception is a problem that arises during the execution of a program. A C++ exception is a response to an exceptional circumstance that arises while a program is running, such as an attempt to divide by zero.

Exceptions provide a way to transfer control from one part of a program to another. C++ exception handling is built upon three keywords: **try, catch,** and **throw**.

- **throw** − A program throws an exception when a problem shows up. This is done using a **throw** keyword.

- **catch** − A program catches an exception with an exception handler at the place in a program where you want to handle the problem. The **catch**keyword indicates the catching of an exception.

- **try** − A **try** block identifies a block of code for which particular exceptions will be activated. It's followed by one or more catch blocks.

Assuming a block will raise an exception, a method catches an exception using a combination of the **try** and **catch** keywords. A try/catch block is placed around the code that might generate an exception. Code within a try/catch block is referred to as protected code, and the syntax for using try/catch as follows −

```
try {
   // protected code
} catch( ExceptionName e1 ) {
   // catch block
} catch( ExceptionName e2 ) {
   // catch block
```

```
} catch( ExceptionName eN ) {
  // catch block
}
```

You can list down multiple **catch** statements to catch different type of exceptions in case your **try** block raises more than one exception in different situations.

Throwing Exceptions

Exceptions can be thrown anywhere within a code block using **throw** statement. The operand of the throw statement determines a type for the exception and can be any expression and the type of the result of the expression determines the type of exception thrown.

Following is an example of throwing an exception when dividing by zero condition occurs −

```
double division(int a, int b) {
  if( b == 0 ) {
    throw "Division by zero condition!";
  }
  return (a/b);
}
```

Catching Exceptions

The **catch** block following the **try** block catches any exception. You can specify what type of exception you want to catch and this is determined by the exception declaration that appears in parentheses following the keyword catch.

```
try {
  // protected code
```

```
} catch( ExceptionName e ) {
 // code to handle ExceptionName exception
}
```

Above code will catch an exception of **ExceptionName** type. If you want to specify that a catch block should handle any type of exception that is thrown in a try block, you must put an ellipsis, ..., between the parentheses enclosing the exception declaration as follows –

```
try {
 // protected code
} catch(...) {
 // code to handle any exception
}
```

The following is an example, which throws a division by zero exception and we catch it in catch block.

```
#include <iostream>
using namespace std;

double division(int a, int b) {
  if( b == 0 ) {
    throw "Division by zero condition!";
  }
  return (a/b);
}

int main () {
  int x = 50;
  int y = 0;
  double z = 0;
```

```
try {
  z = division(x, y);
  cout << z << endl;
} catch (const char* msg) {
  cerr << msg << endl;
}

return 0;
}
```

Because we are raising an exception of type **const char***, so while catching this exception, we have to use const char* in catch block. If we compile and run above code, this would produce the following result −

Division by zero condition!

C++ Standard Exceptions

C++ provides a list of standard exceptions defined in **<exception>** which we can use in our programs. These are arranged in a parent-child class hierarchy shown below –

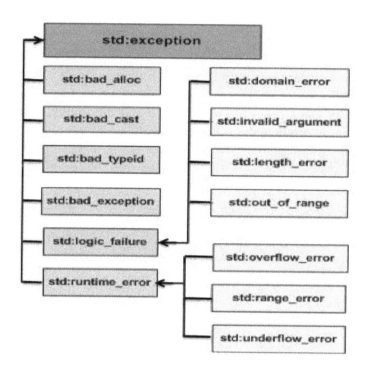

Here is the small description of each exception mentioned in the above hierarchy –

Sr.No	Exception & Description

1	**std::exception** An exception and parent class of all the standard C++ exceptions.
2	**std::bad_alloc** This can be thrown by **new**.
3	**std::bad_cast** This can be thrown by **dynamic_cast**.
4	**std::bad_exception** This is useful device to handle unexpected exceptions in a C++ program.
5	**std::bad_typeid** This can be thrown by **typeid**.
6	**std::logic_error** An exception that theoretically can be detected by reading the code.
7	**std::domain_error** This is an exception thrown when a mathematically invalid domain is used.

8	**std::invalid_argument**
	This is thrown due to invalid arguments.
9	**std::length_error**
	This is thrown when a too big std::string is created.
10	**std::out_of_range**
	This can be thrown by the 'at' method, for example a std::vector and std::bitset<>::operator[]().
11	**std::runtime_error**
	An exception that theoretically cannot be detected by reading the code.
12	**std::overflow_error**
	This is thrown if a mathematical overflow occurs.
13	**std::range_error**
	This is occurred when you try to store a value which is out of range.
14	**std::underflow_error**
	This is thrown if a mathematical underflow

occurs.

Define New Exceptions

You can define your own exceptions by inheriting and overriding **exception** class functionality. Following is the example, which shows how you can use std::exception class to implement your own exception in standard way −

```cpp
#include <iostream>
#include <exception>
using namespace std;

struct MyException : public exception {
  const char * what () const throw () {
    return "C++ Exception";
  }
};

int main() {
  try {
    throw MyException();
  } catch(MyException& e) {
    std::cout << "MyException caught" << std::endl;
    std::cout << e.what() << std::endl;
  } catch(std::exception& e) {
    //Other errors
  }
}
```

This would produce the following result −

MyException caught
C++ Exception

Here, **what()** is a public method provided by exception class and it has been overridden by all the child exception classes. This returns the cause of an exception.

C++ Dynamic Memory

A good understanding of how dynamic memory really works in C++ is essential to becoming a good C++ programmer. Memory in your C++ program is divided into two parts −

- **The stack** − All variables declared inside the function will take up memory from the stack.

- **The heap** − This is unused memory of the program and can be used to allocate the memory dynamically when program runs.

Many times, you are not aware in advance how much memory you will need to store particular information in a defined variable and the size of required memory can be determined at run time.

You can allocate memory at run time within the heap for the variable of a given type using a special operator in C++ which returns the address of the space allocated. This operator is called **new** operator.

If you are not in need of dynamically allocated memory anymore, you can use **delete**operator, which de-allocates memory that was previously allocated by new operator.

new and delete Operators

There is following generic syntax to use **new** operator to allocate memory dynamically for any data-type.

```
new data-type;
```

Here, **data-type** could be any built-in data type including an array or any user defined data types include class or structure. Let us start with built-in data types. For example we can define a pointer to type double and then request that the memory be allocated at execution time. We can do this using the **new** operator with the following statements –

```
double* pvalue  = NULL; // Pointer initialized with null
pvalue  = new double;   // Request memory for the variable
```

The memory may not have been allocated successfully, if the free store had been used up. So it is good practice to check if new operator is returning NULL pointer and take appropriate action as below –

```
double* pvalue  = NULL;
if( !(pvalue  = new double )) {
   cout << "Error: out of memory." <<endl;
   exit(1);
}
```

The **malloc()** function from C, still exists in C++, but it is recommended to avoid using malloc() function. The main advantage of new over malloc() is that new doesn't just allocate memory, it constructs objects which is prime purpose of C++.

At any point, when you feel a variable that has been dynamically allocated is not anymore required, you can free up the memory that it occupies in the free store with the 'delete' operator as follows –

```
delete pvalue;      // Release memory pointed to by pvalue
```

Let us put above concepts and form the following example to show how 'new' and 'delete' work –

```
#include <iostream>
using namespace std;
```

```
int main () {
   double* pvalue  = NULL; // Pointer initialized with null
   pvalue  = new double;    // Request memory for the
variable

   *pvalue = 29494.99;    // Store value at allocated address
   cout << "Value of pvalue : " << *pvalue << endl;

   delete pvalue;        // free up the memory.

   return 0;
}
```

If we compile and run above code, this would produce the following result −

Value of pvalue : 29495

Dynamic Memory Allocation for Arrays

Consider you want to allocate memory for an array of characters, i.e., string of 20 characters. Using the same syntax what we have used above we can allocate memory dynamically as shown below.

```
char* pvalue  = NULL;      // Pointer initialized with null
pvalue  = new char[20];    // Request memory for the
variable
```

To remove the array that we have just created the statement would look like this −

```
delete [] pvalue;          // Delete array pointed to by pvalue
```

Following the similar generic syntax of new operator, you can allocate for a multi-dimensional array as follows −

```
double** pvalue  = NULL;      // Pointer initialized with
null
pvalue  = new double [3][4];  // Allocate memory for a 3x4
array
```

However, the syntax to release the memory for multi-dimensional array will still remain same as above −

```
delete [] pvalue;        // Delete array pointed to by pvalue
```

Dynamic Memory Allocation for Objects

Objects are no different from simple data types. For example, consider the following code where we are going to use an array of objects to clarify the concept −

```cpp
#include <iostream>
using namespace std;

class Box {
  public:
    Box() {
      cout << "Constructor called!" <<endl;
    }
    ~Box() {
      cout << "Destructor called!" <<endl;
    }
};
int main() {
```

```
Box* myBoxArray = new Box[4];
delete [] myBoxArray; // Delete array

return 0;
}
```

If you were to allocate an array of four Box objects, the Simple constructor would be called four times and similarly while deleting these objects, destructor will also be called same number of times.

If we compile and run above code, this would produce the following result −

```
Constructor called!
Constructor called!
Constructor called!
Constructor called!
Destructor called!
Destructor called!
Destructor called!
Destructor called!
```

Namespaces in C++

Consider a situation, when we have two persons with the same name, Zara, in the same class. Whenever we need to differentiate them definitely we would have to use some additional information along with their name, like either the area, if they live in different area or their mother's or father's name, etc.

Same situation can arise in your C++ applications. For example, you might be writing some code that has a function called xyz() and there is another library available which is also having same function xyz(). Now the compiler has no way of knowing which version of xyz() function you are referring to within your code.

A **namespace** is designed to overcome this difficulty and is used as additional information to differentiate similar functions, classes, variables etc. with the same name available in different libraries. Using namespace, you can define the context in which names are defined. In essence, a namespace defines a scope.

Defining a Namespace

A namespace definition begins with the keyword **namespace** followed by the namespace name as follows −

```
namespace namespace_name {
   // code declarations
}
```

To call the namespace-enabled version of either function or variable, prepend (::) the namespace name as follows −

name::code; // code could be variable or function.

Let us see how namespace scope the entities including variable and functions −

```cpp
#include <iostream>
using namespace std;

// first name space
namespace first_space {
  void func() {
    cout << "Inside first_space" << endl;
  }
}

// second name space
namespace second_space {
  void func() {
    cout << "Inside second_space" << endl;
  }
}

int main () {
  // Calls function from first name space.
  first_space::func();

  // Calls function from second name space.
  second_space::func();

  return 0;
}
```

If we compile and run above code, this would produce the following result −

```
Inside first_space
Inside second_space
```

The using directive

You can also avoid prepending of namespaces with the **using namespace** directive. This directive tells the compiler that the subsequent code is making use of names in the specified namespace. The namespace is thus implied for the following code −

```cpp
#include <iostream>
using namespace std;

// first name space
namespace first_space {
  void func() {
    cout << "Inside first_space" << endl;
  }
}

// second name space
namespace second_space {
  void func() {
    cout << "Inside second_space" << endl;
  }
}

using namespace first_space;
int main () {
  // This calls function from first name space.
  func();

  return 0;
}
```

If we compile and run above code, this would produce the following result −

Inside first_space

The 'using' directive can also be used to refer to a particular item within a namespace. For example, if the only part of the std namespace that you intend to use is cout, you can refer to it as follows −

using std::cout;

Subsequent code can refer to cout without prepending the namespace, but other items in the **std** namespace will still need to be explicit as follows −

```cpp
#include <iostream>
using std::cout;

int main () {
   cout << "std::endl is used with std!" << std::endl;

   return 0;
}
```

If we compile and run above code, this would produce the following result −

std::endl is used with std!

Names introduced in a **using** directive obey normal scope rules. The name is visible from the point of the **using** directive to the end of the scope in which the directive is found. Entities with the same name defined in an outer scope are hidden.

Discontiguous Namespaces

A namespace can be defined in several parts and so a namespace is made up of the sum of its separately defined parts. The separate parts of a namespace can be spread over multiple files.

So, if one part of the namespace requires a name defined in another file, that name must still be declared. Writing a following namespace definition either defines a new namespace or adds new elements to an existing one −

```
namespace namespace_name {
  // code declarations
}
```

Nested Namespaces

Namespaces can be nested where you can define one namespace inside another name space as follows −

```
namespace namespace_name1 {
  // code declarations
  namespace namespace_name2 {
    // code declarations
  }
}
```

You can access members of nested namespace by using resolution operators as follows −

```
// to access members of namespace_name2
```

```
using namespace namespace_name1::namespace_name2;

// to access members of namespace:name1
using namespace namespace_name1;
```

In the above statements if you are using namespace_name1, then it will make elements of namespace_name2 available in the scope as follows –

```cpp
#include <iostream>
using namespace std;

// first name space
namespace first_space {
  void func() {
    cout << "Inside first_space" << endl;
  }

  // second name space
  namespace second_space {
    void func() {
      cout << "Inside second_space" << endl;
    }
  }
}

using namespace first_space::second_space;
int main () {
  // This calls function from second name space.
  func();

  return 0;
}
```

If we compile and run above code, this would produce the following result −

```
Inside second_space
```

C++ Templates

Templates are the foundation of generic programming, which involves writing code in a way that is independent of any particular type.

A template is a blueprint or formula for creating a generic class or a function. The library containers like iterators and algorithms are examples of generic programming and have been developed using template concept.

There is a single definition of each container, such as **vector**, but we can define many different kinds of vectors for example, **vector <int>** or **vector <string>**.

You can use templates to define functions as well as classes, let us see how they work −

Function Template

The general form of a template function definition is shown here −

```
template <class type> ret-type func-name(parameter list) {
    // body of function
}
```

Here, type is a placeholder name for a data type used by the function. This name can be used within the function definition.

The following is the example of a function template that returns the maximum of two values −

```
#include <iostream>
#include <string>

using namespace std;
```

```
template <typename T>
inline T const& Max (T const& a, T const& b) {
  return a < b ? b:a;
}

int main () {
  int i = 39;
  int j = 20;
  cout << "Max(i, j): " << Max(i, j) << endl;

  double f1 = 13.5;
  double f2 = 20.7;
  cout << "Max(f1, f2): " << Max(f1, f2) << endl;

  string s1 = "Hello";
  string s2 = "World";
  cout << "Max(s1, s2): " << Max(s1, s2) << endl;

  return 0;
}
```

If we compile and run above code, this would produce the following result –

```
Max(i, j): 39
Max(f1, f2): 20.7
Max(s1, s2): World
```

Class Template

Just as we can define function templates, we can also define class templates. The general form of a generic class declaration is shown here –

```
template <class type> class class-name {
   .
   .
   .
}
```

Here, **type** is the placeholder type name, which will be specified when a class is instantiated. You can define more than one generic data type by using a comma-separated list.

Following is the example to define class Stack<> and implement generic methods to push and pop the elements from the stack −

```
#include <iostream>
#include <vector>
#include <cstdlib>
#include <string>
#include <stdexcept>

using namespace std;

template <class T>
class Stack {
  private:
    vector<T> elems;    // elements

  public:
    void push(T const&); // push element
    void pop();          // pop element
    T top() const;       // return top element

    bool empty() const {     // return true if empty.
      return elems.empty();
    }
```

```cpp
};

template <class T>
void Stack<T>::push (T const& elem) {
  // append copy of passed element
  elems.push_back(elem);
}

template <class T>
void Stack<T>::pop () {
  if (elems.empty()) {
    throw out_of_range("Stack<>::pop(): empty stack");
  }

  // remove last element
  elems.pop_back();
}

template <class T>
T Stack<T>::top () const {
  if (elems.empty()) {
    throw out_of_range("Stack<>::top(): empty stack");
  }

  // return copy of last element
  return elems.back();
}

int main() {
  try {
    Stack<int>      intStack; // stack of ints
    Stack<string> stringStack;   // stack of strings

    // manipulate int stack
    intStack.push(7);
```

```
cout << intStack.top() <<endl;

// manipulate string stack
stringStack.push("hello");
cout << stringStack.top() << std::endl;
stringStack.pop();
stringStack.pop();
} catch (exception const& ex) {
cerr << "Exception: " << ex.what() <<endl;
return -1;
}
}
```

If we compile and run above code, this would produce the following result –

```
7
hello
Exception: Stack<>::pop(): empty stack
```

C++ Preprocessor

The preprocessors are the directives, which give instructions to the compiler to preprocess the information before actual compilation starts.

All preprocessor directives begin with #, and only white-space characters may appear before a preprocessor directive on a line. Preprocessor directives are not C++ statements, so they do not end in a semicolon (;).

You already have seen a **#include** directive in all the examples. This macro is used to include a header file into the source file.

There are number of preprocessor directives supported by C++ like #include, #define, #if, #else, #line, etc. Let us see important directives −

The #define Preprocessor

The #define preprocessor directive creates symbolic constants. The symbolic constant is called a **macro** and the general form of the directive is −

#define macro-name replacement-text

When this line appears in a file, all subsequent occurrences of macro in that file will be replaced by replacement-text before the program is compiled. For example −

```
#include <iostream>
using namespace std;

#define PI 3.14159
```

```
int main () {
  cout << "Value of PI :" << PI << endl;

  return 0;
}
```

Now, let us do the preprocessing of this code to see the result assuming we have the source code file. So let us compile it with -E option and redirect the result to test.p. Now, if you check test.p, it will have lots of information and at the bottom, you will find the value replaced as follows –

```
$gcc -E test.cpp > test.p

...
int main () {
  cout << "Value of PI :" << 3.14159 << endl;
  return 0;
}
```

Function-Like Macros

You can use #define to define a macro which will take argument as follows –

```
#include <iostream>
using namespace std;

#define MIN(a,b) (((a)<(b)) ? a : b)

int main () {
  int i, j;
```

```
   i = 100;
   j = 30;

   cout <<"The minimum is " << MIN(i, j) << endl;

   return 0;
}
```

If we compile and run above code, this would produce the following result −

The minimum is 30

Conditional Compilation

There are several directives, which can be used to compile selective portions of your program's source code. This process is called conditional compilation.

The conditional preprocessor construct is much like the 'if' selection structure. Consider the following preprocessor code −

```
#ifndef NULL
   #define NULL 0
#endif
```

You can compile a program for debugging purpose. You can also turn on or off the debugging using a single macro as follows −

```
#ifdef DEBUG
  cerr <<"Variable x = " << x << endl;
#endif
```

This causes the **cerr** statement to be compiled in the program if the symbolic constant DEBUG has been defined before directive #ifdef DEBUG. You can use #if 0 statment to comment out a portion of the program as follows −

```
#if 0
   code prevented from compiling
#endif
```

Let us try the following example −

```
#include <iostream>
using namespace std;
#define DEBUG

#define MIN(a,b) (((a)<(b)) ? a : b)

int main () {
   int i, j;

   i = 100;
   j = 30;

#ifdef DEBUG
   cerr <<"Trace: Inside main function" << endl;
#endif

#if 0
   /* This is commented part */
   cout << MKSTR(HELLO C++) << endl;
#endif

   cout <<"The minimum is " << MIN(i, j) << endl;
```

```
#ifdef DEBUG
   cerr <<"Trace: Coming out of main function" << endl;
#endif

   return 0;
}
```

If we compile and run above code, this would produce the following result −

```
The minimum is 30
Trace: Inside main function
Trace: Coming out of main function
```

The # and ## Operators

The # and ## preprocessor operators are available in C++ and ANSI/ISO C. The # operator causes a replacement-text token to be converted to a string surrounded by quotes.

Consider the following macro definition −

```
#include <iostream>
using namespace std;

#define MKSTR( x ) #x

int main () {

   cout << MKSTR(HELLO C++) << endl;

   return 0;
}
```

If we compile and run above code, this would produce the following result −

HELLO C++

Let us see how it worked. It is simple to understand that the C++ preprocessor turns the line −

cout << MKSTR(HELLO C++) << endl;

Above line will be turned into the following line −

cout << "HELLO C++" << endl;

The ## operator is used to concatenate two tokens. Here is an example −

#define CONCAT(x, y) x ## y

When CONCAT appears in the program, its arguments are concatenated and used to replace the macro. For example, CONCAT(HELLO, C++) is replaced by "HELLO C++" in the program as follows.

```
#include <iostream>
using namespace std;

#define concat(a, b) a ## b
int main() {
   int xy = 100;

   cout << concat(x, y);
   return 0;
}
```

If we compile and run above code, this would produce the following result −

100

Let us see how it worked. It is simple to understand that the C++ preprocessor transforms −

```
cout << concat(x, y);
```

Above line will be transformed into the following line —

```
cout << xy;
```

Predefined C++ Macros

C++ provides a number of predefined macros mentioned below —

Sr.No	Macro & Description
1	__LINE__ This contains the current line number of the program when it is being compiled.
2	__FILE__ This contains the current file name of the program when it is being compiled.
3	__DATE__ This contains a string of the form month/day/year that is the date of the translation of the source file into object code.

4	__TIME__
	This contains a string of the form hour:minute:second that is the time at which the program was compiled.

Let us see an example for all the above macros −

```
#include <iostream>
using namespace std;

int main () {
   cout << "Value of __LINE__ : " << __LINE__ << endl;
   cout << "Value of __FILE__ : " << __FILE__ << endl;
   cout << "Value of __DATE__ : " << __DATE__ <<
endl;
   cout << "Value of __TIME__ : " << __TIME__ << endl;

   return 0;
}
```

If we compile and run above code, this would produce the following result −

```
Value of __LINE__ : 6
Value of __FILE__ : test.cpp
Value of __DATE__ : Feb 28 2011
Value of __TIME__ : 18:52:48
```

C++ Signal Handling

Signals are the interrupts delivered to a process by the operating system which can terminate a program prematurely. You can generate interrupts by pressing Ctrl+C on a UNIX, LINUX, Mac OS X or Windows system.

There are signals which can not be caught by the program but there is a following list of signals which you can catch in your program and can take appropriate actions based on the signal. These signals are defined in C++ header file <csignal>.

Sr.No	Signal & Description
1	**SIGABRT** Abnormal termination of the program, such as a call to **abort**.
2	**SIGFPE** An erroneous arithmetic operation, such as a divide by zero or an operation resulting in overflow.
3	**SIGILL** Detection of an illegal instruction.

4	**SIGINT** Receipt of an interactive attention signal.
5	**SIGSEGV** An invalid access to storage.
6	**SIGTERM** A termination request sent to the program.

The signal() Function

C++ signal-handling library provides function **signal** to trap unexpected events. Following is the syntax of the signal() function −

```
void (*signal (int sig, void (*func)(int)))(int);
```

Keeping it simple, this function receives two arguments: first argument as an integer which represents signal number and second argument as a pointer to the signal-handling function.

Let us write a simple C++ program where we will catch SIGINT signal using signal() function. Whatever signal you want to catch in your program, you must register that signal using **signal** function and associate it with a signal handler. Examine the following example −

```cpp
#include <iostream>
#include <csignal>

using namespace std;

void signalHandler( int signum ) {
   cout << "Interrupt signal (" << signum << ") received.\n";

   // cleanup and close up stuff here
   // terminate program

   exit(signum);
}

int main () {
   // register signal SIGINT and signal handler
   signal(SIGINT, signalHandler);

   while(1) {
      cout << "Going to sleep...." << endl;
      sleep(1);
   }

   return 0;
}
```

When the above code is compiled and executed, it produces the following result −

```
Going to sleep....
Going to sleep....
Going to sleep....
```

Now, press Ctrl+c to interrupt the program and you will see that your program will catch the signal and would come out by printing something as follows −

```
Going to sleep....
Going to sleep....
Going to sleep....
Interrupt signal (2) received.
```

The raise() Function

You can generate signals by function **raise()**, which takes an integer signal number as an argument and has the following syntax.

```
int raise (signal sig);
```

Here, **sig** is the signal number to send any of the signals: SIGINT, SIGABRT, SIGFPE, SIGILL, SIGSEGV, SIGTERM, SIGHUP.

Following is the example where we raise a signal internally using raise() function as follows −

```cpp
#include <iostream>
#include <csignal>

using namespace std;

void signalHandler( int signum ) {
    cout << "Interrupt signal (" << signum << ") received.\n";

    // cleanup and close up stuff here
    // terminate program

    exit(signum);
}
```

```
int main () {
  int i = 0;
  // register signal SIGINT and signal handler
  signal(SIGINT, signalHandler);

  while(++i) {
    cout << "Going to sleep...." << endl;
    if( i == 3 ) {
      raise( SIGINT);
    }
    sleep(1);
  }

  return 0;
}
```

When the above code is compiled and executed, it produces the following result and would come out automatically –

```
Going to sleep....
Going to sleep....
Going to sleep....
Interrupt signal (2) received.
```

C++ Multithreading

Multithreading is a specialized form of multitasking and a multitasking is the feature that allows your computer to run two or more programs concurrently. In general, there are two types of multitasking: process-based and thread-based.

Process-based multitasking handles the concurrent execution of programs. Thread-based multitasking deals with the concurrent execution of pieces of the same program.

A multithreaded program contains two or more parts that can run concurrently. Each part of such a program is called a thread, and each thread defines a separate path of execution.

C++ does not contain any built-in support for multithreaded applications. Instead, it relies entirely upon the operating system to provide this feature.

This tutorial assumes that you are working on Linux OS and we are going to write multi-threaded C++ program using POSIX. POSIX Threads, or Pthreads provides API which are available on many Unix-like POSIX systems such as FreeBSD, NetBSD, GNU/Linux, Mac OS X and Solaris.

Creating Threads

The following routine is used to create a POSIX thread −

```
#include <pthread.h>
pthread_create (thread, attr, start_routine, arg)
```

Here, **pthread_create** creates a new thread and makes it executable. This routine can be called any number of times from anywhere within your code. Here is the description of the parameters –

Sr.No	Parameter & Description
1	**thread** An opaque, unique identifier for the new thread returned by the subroutine.
2	**attr** An opaque attribute object that may be used to set thread attributes. You can specify a thread attributes object, or NULL for the default values.
3	**start_routine** The C++ routine that the thread will execute once it is created.
4	**arg** A single argument that may be passed to start_routine. It must be passed by reference as a pointer cast of type void. NULL may be used if no argument is to be passed.

The maximum number of threads that may be created by a process is implementation dependent. Once created, threads are peers, and may create other threads. There is no implied hierarchy or dependency between threads.

Terminating Threads

There is following routine which we use to terminate a POSIX thread −

```
#include <pthread.h>
pthread_exit (status)
```

Here **pthread_exit** is used to explicitly exit a thread. Typically, the pthread_exit() routine is called after a thread has completed its work and is no longer required to exist.

If main() finishes before the threads it has created, and exits with pthread_exit(), the other threads will continue to execute. Otherwise, they will be automatically terminated when main() finishes.

Example

This simple example code creates 5 threads with the pthread_create() routine. Each thread prints a "Hello World!" message, and then terminates with a call to pthread_exit().

```
#include <iostream>
#include <cstdlib>
#include <pthread.h>

using namespace std;

#define NUM_THREADS 5
```

```cpp
void *PrintHello(void *threadid) {
  long tid;
  tid = (long)threadid;
  cout << "Hello World! Thread ID, " << tid << endl;
  pthread_exit(NULL);
}

int main () {
  pthread_t threads[NUM_THREADS];
  int rc;
  int i;

  for( i = 0; i < NUM_THREADS; i++ ) {
    cout << "main() : creating thread, " << i << endl;
    rc = pthread_create(&threads[i], NULL, PrintHello,
(void *)i);

    if (rc) {
      cout << "Error:unable to create thread," << rc <<
endl;
      exit(-1);
    }
  }
  pthread_exit(NULL);
}
```

Compile the following program using -lpthread library as follows –

```
$gcc test.cpp -lpthread
```

Now, execute your program which gives the following output –

```
main() : creating thread, 0
main() : creating thread, 1
main() : creating thread, 2
main() : creating thread, 3
main() : creating thread, 4
Hello World! Thread ID, 0
Hello World! Thread ID, 1
Hello World! Thread ID, 2
Hello World! Thread ID, 3
Hello World! Thread ID, 4
```

Passing Arguments to Threads

This example shows how to pass multiple arguments via a structure. You can pass any data type in a thread callback because it points to void as explained in the following example −

```cpp
#include <iostream>
#include <cstdlib>
#include <pthread.h>

using namespace std;

#define NUM_THREADS 5

struct thread_data {
   int thread_id;
   char *message;
};

void *PrintHello(void *threadarg) {
```

```
    struct thread_data *my_data;
    my_data = (struct thread_data *) threadarg;

    cout << "Thread ID : " << my_data->thread_id ;
    cout << " Message : " << my_data->message << endl;

    pthread_exit(NULL);
}

int main () {
    pthread_t threads[NUM_THREADS];
    struct thread_data td[NUM_THREADS];
    int rc;
    int i;

    for( i = 0; i < NUM_THREADS; i++ ) {
        cout <<"main() : creating thread, " << i << endl;
        td[i].thread_id = i;
        td[i].message = "This is message";
        rc = pthread_create(&threads[i], NULL, PrintHello,
(void *)&td[i]);

        if (rc) {
            cout << "Error:unable to create thread," << rc <<
endl;
            exit(-1);
        }
    }
    pthread_exit(NULL);
}
```

When the above code is compiled and executed, it produces the following result −

```
main() : creating thread, 0
main() : creating thread, 1
main() : creating thread, 2
main() : creating thread, 3
main() : creating thread, 4
Thread ID : 3 Message : This is message
Thread ID : 2 Message : This is message
Thread ID : 0 Message : This is message
Thread ID : 1 Message : This is message
Thread ID : 4 Message : This is message
```

Joining and Detaching Threads

There are following two routines which we can use to join or detach threads −

```
pthread_join (threadid, status)
pthread_detach (threadid)
```

The pthread_join() subroutine blocks the calling thread until the specified 'threadid' thread terminates. When a thread is created, one of its attributes defines whether it is joinable or detached. Only threads that are created as joinable can be joined. If a thread is created as detached, it can never be joined.

This example demonstrates how to wait for thread completions by using the Pthread join routine.

```cpp
#include <iostream>
#include <cstdlib>
#include <pthread.h>
```

```cpp
#include <unistd.h>

using namespace std;

#define NUM_THREADS 5

void *wait(void *t) {
   int i;
   long tid;

   tid = (long)t;

   sleep(1);
   cout << "Sleeping in thread " << endl;
   cout << "Thread with id : " << tid << "  ...exiting " << endl;
   pthread_exit(NULL);
}

int main () {
   int rc;
   int i;
   pthread_t threads[NUM_THREADS];
   pthread_attr_t attr;
   void *status;

   // Initialize and set thread joinable
   pthread_attr_init(&attr);
   pthread_attr_setdetachstate(&attr,
PTHREAD_CREATE_JOINABLE);

   for( i = 0; i < NUM_THREADS; i++ ) {
      cout << "main() : creating thread, " << i << endl;
      rc = pthread_create(&threads[i], &attr, wait, (void *)i );
```

```
    if (rc) {
        cout << "Error:unable to create thread," << rc <<
endl;
        exit(-1);
        }
    }

    // free attribute and wait for the other threads
    pthread_attr_destroy(&attr);
    for( i = 0; i < NUM_THREADS; i++ ) {
        rc = pthread_join(threads[i], &status);
        if (rc) {
            cout << "Error:unable to join," << rc << endl;
            exit(-1);
        }

        cout << "Main: completed thread id :" << i ;
        cout << " exiting with status :" << status << endl;
    }

    cout << "Main: program exiting." << endl;
    pthread_exit(NULL);
}
```

When the above code is compiled and executed, it produces the following result −

```
main() : creating thread, 0
main() : creating thread, 1
main() : creating thread, 2
main() : creating thread, 3
main() : creating thread, 4
Sleeping in thread
```

```
Thread with id : 0 .... exiting
Sleeping in thread
Thread with id : 1 .... exiting
Sleeping in thread
Thread with id : 2 .... exiting
Sleeping in thread
Thread with id : 3 .... exiting
Sleeping in thread
Thread with id : 4 .... exiting
Main: completed thread id :0  exiting with status :0
Main: completed thread id :1  exiting with status :0
Main: completed thread id :2  exiting with status :0
Main: completed thread id :3  exiting with status :0
Main: completed thread id :4  exiting with status :0
Main: program exiting.
```

C++ Web Programming

What is CGI?

- The Common Gateway Interface, or CGI, is a set of standards that define how information is exchanged between the web server and a custom script.

- The CGI specs are currently maintained by the NCSA and NCSA defines CGI is as follows –

- The Common Gateway Interface, or CGI, is a standard for external gateway programs to interface with information servers such as HTTP servers.

- The current version is CGI/1.1 and CGI/1.2 is under progress.

Web Browsing

To understand the concept of CGI, let's see what happens when we click a hyperlink to browse a particular web page or URL.

- Your browser contacts the HTTP web server and demand for the URL ie. filename.

- Web Server will parse the URL and will look for the filename. If it finds requested file then web server sends that file back to the browser otherwise sends an error message indicating that you have requested a wrong file.

- Web browser takes response from web server and displays either the received file or error message based on the received response.

However, it is possible to set up the HTTP server in such a way that whenever a file in a certain directory is requested, that file is not sent back; instead it is executed as a program, and produced output from the program is sent back to your browser to display.

The Common Gateway Interface (CGI) is a standard protocol for enabling applications (called CGI programs or CGI scripts) to interact with Web servers and with clients. These CGI programs can be a written in Python, PERL, Shell, C or C++ etc.

CGI Architecture Diagram

The following simple program shows a simple architecture of CGI −

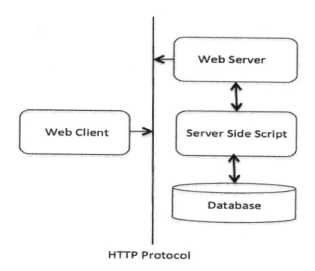

Web Server Configuration

Before you proceed with CGI Programming, make sure that your Web Server supports CGI and it is configured to handle CGI Programs. All the CGI Programs to be executed by the HTTP server are kept in a pre-configured directory. This directory is called CGI directory and by convention it is named as /var/www/cgi-bin. By convention CGI files will have extension as **.cgi**, though they are C++ executable.

By default, Apache Web Server is configured to run CGI programs in /var/www/cgi-bin. If you want to specify any other directory to run your CGI scripts, you can modify the following section in the httpd.conf file −

```
<Directory "/var/www/cgi-bin">
   AllowOverride None
   Options ExecCGI
   Order allow,deny
   Allow from all
</Directory>

<Directory "/var/www/cgi-bin">
   Options All
</Directory>
```

Here, I assume that you have Web Server up and running successfully and you are able to run any other CGI program like Perl or Shell etc.

First CGI Program

Consider the following C++ Program content −

```
#include <iostream>
using namespace std;

int main () {
  cout << "Content-type:text/html\r\n\r\n";
  cout << "<html>\n";
  cout << "<head>\n";
  cout << "<title>Hello World - First CGI Program</title>\n";
  cout << "</head>\n";
  cout << "<body>\n";
  cout << "<h2>Hello World! This is my first CGI program</h2>\n";
  cout << "</body>\n";
  cout << "</html>\n";

  return 0;
}
```

Compile above code and name the executable as cplusplus.cgi. This file is being kept in /var/www/cgi-bin directory and it has following content. Before running your CGI program make sure you have change mode of file using **chmod 755 cplusplus.cgi**UNIX command to make file executable.

My First CGI program

The above C++ program is a simple program which is writing its output on STDOUT file i.e. screen. There is one important and extra feature available which is first line printing **Content-type:text/html\r\n\r\n**. This line is sent back to the browser and specify the content type to be displayed on the browser screen. Now you must have understood the basic concept of CGI and you can write many complicated CGI programs using Python. A C++ CGI program can interact with any other external system, such as RDBMS, to exchange information.

HTTP Header

The line **Content-type:text/html\r\n\r\n** is a part of HTTP header, which is sent to the browser to understand the content. All the HTTP header will be in the following form −

HTTP Field Name: Field Content

For Example
Content-type: text/html\r\n\r\n

There are few other important HTTP headers, which you will use frequently in your CGI Programming.

Sr.No	Header & Description
1	**Content-type:** A MIME string defining the format of the file being returned. Example is Content-type:text/html.
2	**Expires: Date** The date the information becomes invalid. This should be used by the browser to decide when a page needs to be refreshed. A valid date string

	should be in the format 01 Jan 1998 12:00:00 GMT.
3	**Location: URL** The URL that should be returned instead of the URL requested. You can use this filed to redirect a request to any file.
4	**Last-modified: Date** The date of last modification of the resource.
5	**Content-length: N** The length, in bytes, of the data being returned. The browser uses this value to report the estimated download time for a file.
6	**Set-Cookie: String** Set the cookie passed through the *string*.

CGI Environment Variables

All the CGI program will have access to the following environment variables. These variables play an important role while writing any CGI program.

Sr.No	Variable Name & Description
1	**CONTENT_TYPE** The data type of the content, used when the client is sending attached content to the server. For example file upload etc.
2	**CONTENT_LENGTH** The length of the query information that is available only for POST requests.
3	**HTTP_COOKIE** Returns the set cookies in the form of key & value pair.
4	**HTTP_USER_AGENT** The User-Agent request-header field contains information about the user agent originating the request. It is a name of the web browser.
5	**PATH_INFO** The path for the CGI script.
6	**QUERY_STRING** The URL-encoded information that is sent with

	GET method request.
7	**REMOTE_ADDR** The IP address of the remote host making the request. This can be useful for logging or for authentication purpose.
8	**REMOTE_HOST** The fully qualified name of the host making the request. If this information is not available then REMOTE_ADDR can be used to get IR address.
9	**REQUEST_METHOD** The method used to make the request. The most common methods are GET and POST.
10	**SCRIPT_FILENAME** The full path to the CGI script.
11	**SCRIPT_NAME** The name of the CGI script.
12	**SERVER_NAME** The server's hostname or IP Address.

13	**SERVER_SOFTWARE**
	The name and version of the software the server is running.

Here is small CGI program to list out all the CGI variables.

```cpp
#include <iostream>
#include <stdlib.h>
using namespace std;

const string ENV[ 24 ] = {
  "COMSPEC",                  "DOCUMENT_ROOT",
"GATEWAY_INTERFACE",
  "HTTP_ACCEPT", "HTTP_ACCEPT_ENCODING",
  "HTTP_ACCEPT_LANGUAGE",
"HTTP_CONNECTION",
  "HTTP_HOST", "HTTP_USER_AGENT", "PATH",
  "QUERY_STRING",                "REMOTE_ADDR",
"REMOTE_PORT",
  "REQUEST_METHOD",             "REQUEST_URI",
"SCRIPT_FILENAME",
  "SCRIPT_NAME",                "SERVER_ADDR",
"SERVER_ADMIN",

  "SERVER_NAME","SERVER_PORT","SERVER_PROT
OCOL",
  "SERVER_SIGNATURE","SERVER_SOFTWARE" };

int main () {
  cout << "Content-type:text/html\r\n\r\n";
  cout << "<html>\n";
```

```cpp
   cout << "<head>\n";
   cout << "<title>CGI Environment Variables</title>\n";
   cout << "</head>\n";
   cout << "<body>\n";
   cout << "<table border = \"0\" cellspacing = \"2\">";

for ( int i = 0; i < 24; i++ ) {
   cout << "<tr><td>" << ENV[ i ] << "</td><td>";

   // attempt to retrieve value of environment variable
   char *value = getenv( ENV[ i ].c_str() );
   if ( value != 0 ) {
     cout << value;
   } else {
     cout << "Environment variable does not exist.";
   }
   cout << "</td></tr>\n";
}

cout << "</table><\n";
cout << "</body>\n";
cout << "</html>\n";

return 0;
}
```

C++ CGI Library

For real examples, you would need to do many operations by your CGI program. There is a CGI library written for C++ program which you can download from ftp://ftp.gnu.org/gnu/cgicc/ and follow the steps to install the library −

```
$tar xzf cgicc-X.X.X.tar.gz
$cd cgicc-X.X.X/
$./configure --prefix=/usr
$make
$make install
```

You can check related documentation available at 'C++ CGI Lib Documentation.

GET and POST Methods

You must have come across many situations when you need to pass some information from your browser to web server and ultimately to your CGI Program. Most frequently browser uses two methods to pass this information to web server. These methods are GET Method and POST Method.

Passing Information Using GET Method

The GET method sends the encoded user information appended to the page request. The page and the encoded information are separated by the ? character as follows −

```
http://www.test.com/cgi-
bin/cpp.cgi?key1=value1&key2=value2
```

The GET method is the default method to pass information from browser to web server and it produces a long string that appears in your browser's Location:box. Never use the GET method if you have password or other sensitive information to pass to the server. The GET method has size limitation and you can pass upto 1024 characters in a request string.

When using GET method, information is passed using QUERY_STRING http header and will be accessible in your CGI Program through QUERY_STRING environment variable.

You can pass information by simply concatenating key and value pairs alongwith any URL or you can use HTML <FORM> tags to pass information using GET method.

Simple URL Example: Get Method

Here is a simple URL which will pass two values to hello_get.py program using GET method.

/cgi-bin/cpp_get.cgi?first_name=ZARA&last_name=ALI

Below is a program to generate **cpp_get.cgi** CGI program to handle input given by web browser. We are going to use C++ CGI library which makes it very easy to access passed information −

```cpp
#include <iostream>
#include <vector>
#include <string>
#include <stdio.h>
#include <stdlib.h>

#include <cgicc/CgiDefs.h>
#include <cgicc/Cgicc.h>
```

```cpp
#include <cgicc/HTTPHTMLHeader.h>
#include <cgicc/HTMLClasses.h>

using namespace std;
using namespace cgicc;

int main () {
  Cgicc formData;

  cout << "Content-type:text/html\r\n\r\n";
  cout << "<html>\n";
  cout << "<head>\n";
  cout << "<title>Using GET and POST Methods</title>\n";
  cout << "</head>\n";
  cout << "<body>\n";

  form_iterator fi = formData.getElement("first_name");
  if( !fi->isEmpty() && fi != (*formData).end()) {
    cout << "First name: " << **fi << endl;
  } else {
    cout << "No text entered for first name" << endl;
  }

  cout << "<br/>\n";
  fi = formData.getElement("last_name");
  if( !fi->isEmpty() &&fi != (*formData).end()) {
    cout << "Last name: " << **fi << endl;
  } else {
    cout << "No text entered for last name" << endl;
  }

  cout << "<br/>\n";
  cout << "</body>\n";
  cout << "</html>\n";
```

```
    return 0;
}
```

Now, compile the above program as follows −

```
$g++ -o cpp_get.cgi cpp_get.cpp -lcgicc
```

Generate cpp_get.cgi and put it in your CGI directory and try to access using following link −

```
/cgi-bin/cpp_get.cgi?first_name=ZARA&last_name=ALI
```

This would generate following result −

```
First name: ZARA
Last name: ALI
```

Simple FORM Example: GET Method

Here is a simple example which passes two values using HTML FORM and submit button. We are going to use same CGI script cpp_get.cgi to handle this input.

```
<form action = "/cgi-bin/cpp_get.cgi" method = "get">
  First Name: <input type = "text" name = "first_name">
<br />

  Last Name: <input type = "text" name = "last_name" />
  <input type = "submit" value = "Submit" />
</form>
```

Passing Information Using POST Method

A generally more reliable method of passing information to a CGI program is the POST method. This packages the information in exactly the same way as GET methods, but instead of sending it as a text string after a ? in the URL it sends it as a separate message. This message comes into the CGI script in the form of the standard input.

The same cpp_get.cgi program will handle POST method as well. Let us take same example as above, which passes two values using HTML FORM and submit button but this time with POST method as follows −

```
<form action = "/cgi-bin/cpp_get.cgi" method = "post">
   First   Name:   <input   type   =   "text"   name   =
"first_name"><br />
   Last Name: <input type = "text" name = "last_name" />

   <input type = "submit" value = "Submit" />
</form>
```

Passing Checkbox Data to CGI Program

Checkboxes are used when more than one option is required to be selected.

Here is example HTML code for a form with two checkboxes −

```
<form   action   =   "/cgi-bin/cpp_checkbox.cgi"   method   =
"POST" target = "_blank">
   <input type = "checkbox" name = "maths" value = "on"
/> Maths
```

```
   <input type = "checkbox" name = "physics" value = "on"
/> Physics
   <input type = "submit" value = "Select Subject" />
</form>
```

The result of this code is the following form −

Below is C++ program, which will generate cpp_checkbox.cgi script to handle input given by web browser through checkbox button.

```cpp
#include <iostream>
#include <vector>
#include <string>
#include <stdio.h>
#include <stdlib.h>

#include <cgicc/CgiDefs.h>
#include <cgicc/Cgicc.h>
#include <cgicc/HTTPHTMLHeader.h>
#include <cgicc/HTMLClasses.h>

using namespace std;
using namespace cgicc;

int main () {
  Cgicc formData;
  bool maths_flag, physics_flag;

  cout << "Content-type:text/html\r\n\r\n";
  cout << "<html>\n";
```

```
cout << "<head>\n";
cout << "<title>Checkbox Data to CGI</title>\n";
cout << "</head>\n";
cout << "<body>\n";

maths_flag = formData.queryCheckbox("maths");
if( maths_flag ) {
   cout << "Maths Flag: ON " << endl;
} else {
   cout << "Maths Flag: OFF " << endl;
}
cout << "<br/>\n";

physics_flag = formData.queryCheckbox("physics");
if( physics_flag ) {
   cout << "Physics Flag: ON " << endl;
} else {
   cout << "Physics Flag: OFF " << endl;
}

cout << "<br/>\n";
cout << "</body>\n";
cout << "</html>\n";

return 0;

}
```

Passing Radio Button Data to CGI Program

Radio Buttons are used when only one option is required
to be selected.

Here is example HTML code for a form with two radio button −

```
<form action = "/cgi-bin/cpp_radiobutton.cgi" method =
"post" target = "_blank">
   <input type = "radio" name = "subject" value = "maths"
checked = "checked"/> Maths
   <input type = "radio" name = "subject" value = "physics"
/> Physics
   <input type = "submit" value = "Select Subject" />
</form>
```

The result of this code is the following form −

Below is C++ program, which will generate cpp_radiobutton.cgi script to handle input given by web browser through radio buttons.

```cpp
#include <iostream>
#include <vector>
#include <string>
#include <stdio.h>
#include <stdlib.h>

#include <cgicc/CgiDefs.h>
#include <cgicc/Cgicc.h>
#include <cgicc/HTTPHTMLHeader.h>
#include <cgicc/HTMLClasses.h>

using namespace std;
using namespace cgicc;
```

```
int main () {
  Cgicc formData;

  cout << "Content-type:text/html\r\n\r\n";
  cout << "<html>\n";
  cout << "<head>\n";
  cout << "<title>Radio Button Data to CGI</title>\n";
  cout << "</head>\n";
  cout << "<body>\n";

  form_iterator fi = formData.getElement("subject");
  if( !fi->isEmpty() && fi != (*formData).end()) {
    cout << "Radio box selected: " << **fi << endl;
  }

  cout << "<br/>\n";
  cout << "</body>\n";
  cout << "</html>\n";

  return 0;
}
```

Passing Text Area Data to CGI Program

TEXTAREA element is used when multiline text has to be passed to the CGI Program.

Here is example HTML code for a form with a TEXTAREA box −

```
<form action = "/cgi-bin/cpp_textarea.cgi" method = "post"
target = "_blank">
```

```
<textarea name = "textcontent" cols = "40" rows = "4">
   Type your text here...
</textarea>
<input type = "submit" value = "Submit" />
</form>
```

The result of this code is the following form −

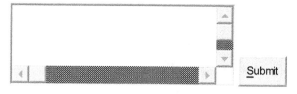

Below is C++ program, which will generate cpp_textarea.cgi script to handle input given by web browser through text area.

```
#include <iostream>
#include <vector>
#include <string>
#include <stdio.h>
#include <stdlib.h>

#include <cgicc/CgiDefs.h>
#include <cgicc/Cgicc.h>
#include <cgicc/HTTPHTMLHeader.h>
#include <cgicc/HTMLClasses.h>

using namespace std;
using namespace cgicc;

int main () {
  Cgicc formData;
```

```cpp
cout << "Content-type:text/html\r\n\r\n";
cout << "<html>\n";
cout << "<head>\n";
cout << "<title>Text Area Data to CGI</title>\n";
cout << "</head>\n";
cout << "<body>\n";

form_iterator fi = formData.getElement("textcontent");
if( !fi->isEmpty() && fi != (*formData).end()) {
  cout << "Text Content: " << **fi << endl;
} else {
  cout << "No text entered" << endl;
}

cout << "<br/>\n";
cout << "</body>\n";
cout << "</html>\n";

return 0;
}
```

Passing Drop down Box Data to CGI Program

Drop down Box is used when we have many options available but only one or two will be selected.

Here is example HTML code for a form with one drop down box −

```html
<form action = "/cgi-bin/cpp_dropdown.cgi" method = "post" target = "_blank">
  <select name = "dropdown">
```

```
<option value = "Maths" selected>Maths</option>
<option value = "Physics">Physics</option>
</select>

<input type = "submit" value = "Submit"/>
</form>
```

The result of this code is the following form −

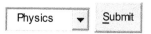

Below is C++ program, which will generate cpp_dropdown.cgi script to handle input given by web browser through drop down box.

```cpp
#include <iostream>
#include <vector>
#include <string>
#include <stdio.h>
#include <stdlib.h>

#include <cgicc/CgiDefs.h>
#include <cgicc/Cgicc.h>
#include <cgicc/HTTPHTMLHeader.h>
#include <cgicc/HTMLClasses.h>

using namespace std;
using namespace cgicc;

int main () {
  Cgicc formData;

  cout << "Content-type:text/html\r\n\r\n";
  cout << "<html>\n";
```

```
cout << "<head>\n";
cout << "<title>Drop Down Box Data to CGI</title>\n";
cout << "</head>\n";
cout << "<body>\n";

form_iterator fi = formData.getElement("dropdown");
if( !fi->isEmpty() && fi != (*formData).end()) {
    cout << "Value Selected: " << **fi << endl;
}

cout << "<br/>\n";
cout << "</body>\n";
cout << "</html>\n";

return 0;
}
```

Using Cookies in CGI

HTTP protocol is a stateless protocol. But for a commercial website it is required to maintain session information among different pages. For example one user registration ends after completing many pages. But how to maintain user's session information across all the web pages.

In many situations, using cookies is the most efficient method of remembering and tracking preferences, purchases, commissions, and other information required for better visitor experience or site statistics.

How It Works

Your server sends some data to the visitor's browser in the form of a cookie. The browser may accept the cookie. If it does, it is stored as a plain text record on the visitor's hard drive. Now, when the visitor arrives at another page on your site, the cookie is available for retrieval. Once retrieved, your server knows/remembers what was stored.

Cookies are a plain text data record of 5 variable-length fields –

- **Expires** – This shows date the cookie will expire. If this is blank, the cookie will expire when the visitor quits the browser.

- **Domain** – This shows domain name of your site.

- **Path** – This shows path to the directory or web page that set the cookie. This may be blank if you want to retrieve the cookie from any directory or page.

- **Secure** – If this field contains the word "secure" then the cookie may only be retrieved with a secure server. If this field is blank, no such restriction exists.

- **Name = Value** – Cookies are set and retrieved in the form of key and value pairs.

Setting up Cookies

It is very easy to send cookies to browser. These cookies will be sent along with HTTP Header before the Content-type filed. Assuming you want to set UserID and

Password as cookies. So cookies setting will be done as follows

```cpp
#include <iostream>
using namespace std;

int main () {
  cout << "Set-Cookie:UserID = XYZ;\r\n";
  cout << "Set-Cookie:Password = XYZ123;\r\n";
  cout << "Set-Cookie:Domain = www.google.com;\r\n";
  cout << "Set-Cookie:Path = /perl;\n";
  cout << "Content-type:text/html\r\n\r\n";

  cout << "<html>\n";
  cout << "<head>\n";
  cout << "<title>Cookies in CGI</title>\n";
  cout << "</head>\n";
  cout << "<body>\n";

  cout << "Setting cookies" << endl;

  cout << "<br/>\n";
  cout << "</body>\n";
  cout << "</html>\n";

  return 0;
}
```

From this example, you must have understood how to set cookies. We use **Set-Cookie**HTTP header to set cookies.

Here, it is optional to set cookies attributes like Expires, Domain, and Path. It is notable that cookies are set before sending magic line **"Content-type:text/html\r\n\r\n**.

Compile above program to produce setcookies.cgi, and try to set cookies using following link. It will set four cookies at your computer –

/cgi-bin/setcookies.cgi

Retrieving Cookies

It is easy to retrieve all the set cookies. Cookies are stored in CGI environment variable HTTP_COOKIE and they will have following form.

key1 = value1; key2 = value2; key3 = value3....

Here is an example of how to retrieve cookies.

```cpp
#include <iostream>
#include <vector>
#include <string>
#include <stdio.h>
#include <stdlib.h>

#include <cgicc/CgiDefs.h>
#include <cgicc/Cgicc.h>
#include <cgicc/HTTPHTMLHeader.h>
#include <cgicc/HTMLClasses.h>

using namespace std;
using namespace cgicc;

int main () {
  Cgicc cgi;
  const_cookie_iterator cci;
```

```
cout << "Content-type:text/html\r\n\r\n";
cout << "<html>\n";
cout << "<head>\n";
cout << "<title>Cookies in CGI</title>\n";
cout << "</head>\n";
cout << "<body>\n";
cout << "<table border = \"0\" cellspacing = \"2\">";

// get environment variables
const CgiEnvironment& env = cgi.getEnvironment();

for( cci = env.getCookieList().begin();
cci != env.getCookieList().end();
++cci ) {
   cout    <<    "<tr><td>"   <<   cci->getName()   <<
"</td><td>";
   cout << cci->getValue();
   cout << "</td></tr>\n";
}

cout << "</table><\n";
cout << "<br/>\n";
cout << "</body>\n";
cout << "</html>\n";

return 0;
}
```

Now, compile above program to produce getcookies.cgi, and try to get a list of all the cookies available at your computer −

/cgi-bin/getcookies.cgi

This will produce a list of all the four cookies set in previous section and all other cookies set in your computer –

UserID XYZ
Password XYZ123
Domain www.google.com
Path /perl

File Upload Example

To upload a file the HTML form must have the enctype attribute set to **multipart/form-data**. The input tag with the file type will create a "Browse" button.

```
<html>
 <body>
   <form enctype = "multipart/form-data" action = "/cgi-
bin/cpp_uploadfile.cgi"
     method = "post">
     <p>File: <input type = "file" name = "userfile"
/></p>
     <p><input type = "submit" value = "Upload" /></p>
   </form>
 </body>
</html>
```

The result of this code is the following form –

File:

Upload

Here is the script **cpp_uploadfile.cpp** to handle file upload −

```
#include <iostream>
#include <vector>
#include <string>
#include <stdio.h>
#include <stdlib.h>

#include <cgicc/CgiDefs.h>
#include <cgicc/Cgicc.h>
#include <cgicc/HTTPHTMLHeader.h>
#include <cgicc/HTMLClasses.h>

using namespace std;
using namespace cgicc;

int main () {
  Cgicc cgi;

  cout << "Content-type:text/html\r\n\r\n";
  cout << "<html>\n";
  cout << "<head>\n";
  cout << "<title>File Upload in CGI</title>\n";
  cout << "</head>\n";
  cout << "<body>\n";

  // get list of files to be uploaded
  const_file_iterator file = cgi.getFile("userfile");
  if(file != cgi.getFiles().end()) {
    // send data type at cout.
    cout << HTTPContentHeader(file->getDataType());
    // write content at cout.
    file->writeToStream(cout);
  }
```

```
cout << "<File uploaded successfully>\n";
cout << "</body>\n";
cout << "</html>\n";

return 0;
}
```

The above example is for writing content at **cout** stream but you can open your file stream and save the content of uploaded file in a file at desired location.

Thank You!